The
LO²LA Principle

The
LO²LA Principle

The Perfectness of the World

René Egli

Be Like An Apple Tree

ISBN: 979-8-9936991-0-3

Book design by Olivier Bernard Egli

BY RENÉ EGLI

Available in English

The Solution: A Manifesto (co-authored with Françoise Egli)
The LO²LA Principle: The Perfectness of the World

Available in German only

Illusion or Reality: The Practical Application of the LO²LA Principle
The LO²LA Principle: The Formula for Wealth
The LO²LA Principle: An Exploration of Zero Time
20 Years of the LO²LA Principle: It is as it is. Full Stop.
The Teaching of the Perfectness of the World: A Reference Guide

"The world, friend Govinda, is not imperfect, or on a slow path to perfection: no, it is perfect at every moment."
—Hermann Hesse, Siddhartha

"It is my opinion that everything must be based on a simple idea. And it is my opinion that this idea, once we have finally discovered it, will be so compelling, so beautiful, that we will say to one another, yes, how could it have been any different."
—John Archibald Wheeler, Theoretical Physicist

Table of Contents

Author's Note

When I began writing this book over thirty years ago, my goal was to summarize what I call universal laws. Even as a young man, I kept asking myself, *How does life work?* Libraries are full of books explaining how people, cars, computers, or businesses function. What about life? Everyone has to live it, so how does it work?

I thought, *Every human being should receive some kind of user manual for life at birth.* So, I sat down and wrote one, first and foremost, for myself. I never would have imagined that this book would still be finding its way to readers thirty years later.

But then again, universal laws don't change. Science may evolve, but those laws were as valid one thousand years ago as they are today, and they'll still be valid one thousand years from now.

—René Egli, 2025

Introduction I

A speck of dust drifts through the vastness of the cosmos, one among billions. Its inhabitants have named it "Planet Earth."

For thousands of years, something peculiar has been happening on this little grain of cosmic matter. The beings who live there, who call themselves humans, spend much of their time in conflict with one another. Sometimes, these conflicts escalate to a point resulting in death. What's striking is that, from an outside perspective, these acts seem senseless. It's never about controlling the entire planet. More often than not, it's about gaining power over a tiny sliver of it, barely a fraction of the dust they inhabit.

Even more baffling is that for most of their history, humans believed they were the only beings in the universe. Despite not fully understanding how the cosmos works, they crowned themselves as the pinnacle of creation. Some still cling to this idea today. There are even theories suggesting that humans are inherently aggressive, that conflict, war, and violence are part of human nature and will always be with us.

But let's keep this in perspective. If Earth truly is a speck of dust in the infinity of space, then it's not hard to imagine the following scenario: every few hundred or thousand years (which is barely a blink in cosmic time), more advanced beings pass by to check in. Their intention? To see if humanity has finally begun to understand how this thing called 'life' actually works. So far, these cosmic visitors would likely have left Earth shaking their heads, puzzled by humanity's stubborn refusal to understand what, from their perspective, must be pretty straightforward: Why doesn't the human mind work in harmony with the laws of life?

That question is precisely what this book seeks to explore. What you are holding in your hands is a guide to life, an operating manual. We have manuals for everything these days, including cars, washing machines, and smartphones. Here is a manual for the one thing we all have to "operate" every single day: Life itself.

What if there is no natural law that says we must fight, suffer, or destroy?

What if life is not a constant series of struggles, large or small?

What if there are universal laws, simple but powerful, that we continually violate, making life more difficult than it needs to be?

The LO²LA Principle may point toward a path through and out of many of those difficulties. The only way to know is to test it for yourself and experiment with it. If you do, you may discover something profound and may come to understand what Hermann Hesse meant when he wrote in Siddhartha: "The world, friend Govinda, is not imperfect, or on a slow path to perfection: no, it is perfect at every moment."

The challenge isn't to fix the world. The challenge is to see it and yourself more clearly. Perhaps then, life can begin to work as it was always meant to.

Introduction II

Whenever someone talks about wisdom teachings or laws of life, we often think of the East, specifically spiritual masters, gurus, or ancient philosophers from India, China, or Japan. And it's true: those traditions have produced extraordinary insights, and they continue to inspire many. However, for this book, I'd like to clarify two important things. First, I make no distinction between "Eastern" and "Western" wisdom. If something truly qualifies as a law of life, then by definition, it must apply everywhere. It must work in New York just as it does in Mumbai. A universal law doesn't need cultural context to be true. Second, my approach is grounded in a perspective that's perhaps a bit different from traditional wisdom teachings: I come to this subject as an economist. That might sound unusual, but it's central to The LO^{2}LA Principle. I'm interested not only in whether an idea is inspiring or spiritually rich, but also in whether it actually works efficiently and practically in our daily lives, including in business, relationships, and decision-making.

As a Westerner and economist, I'll be honest: I find it difficult to sit cross-legged for hours repeating mantras or meditating on "nothingness" for years on end. I admire the discipline of those who do, but I question whether that approach is realistic, or even necessary, for most people, especially in the fast-paced Western world. In fact, many traditional spiritual practices often seem designed for a select few who have the time, space, and privilege to pursue them. And yet, solving life's challenges shouldn't be reserved for the few. Everyone, in every walk of life, should have access to a principle that helps them improve their lives now—not years from now.

That's why I believe we need a behavioral framework. Something simple. Something that can be applied immediately, without requiring long spiritual training or a deep background in philosophy, science, or theology. The only real requirement is common sense. And sadly, common sense is often obscured by excessive academic or intellectual knowledge. Sometimes, the more we know, the harder it becomes to see the simple truths right in front of us.

My goal with this book is to present a principle—a way of thinking and acting—that anyone can try out immediately in their own life. You don't have to believe in it ahead of time. You don't have to debate it or argue over its origins. Just test it. Try it for yourself. Observe the results. It isn't a theory, and it's not about abstract philosophy. It is about behavior in our daily lives.

What Matters in Life

It is said that the Buddha dismissed the question of God as just a theory. So, if that's not the question, then what is? What actually matters? In my opinion, that's the question we especially need to ask ourselves here in the West. Because there's something I constantly hear from people: "I have no time!" If we really believe we don't have enough time, then wouldn't it make sense to focus on what matters most? To give our attention to what (and this is the economist in me speaking) brings the highest return for the time and energy we invest? Strangely, many people don't even have time for that.

To put it in the form of a simple story:

A man sits at the edge of a lake trying to catch fish with his bare hands. A traveler walks by, watches for a moment, then gently pats him on the shoulder and says, "Hey, friend, let me show you how to make a net. You'll catch far more fish, much faster." But the man doesn't even look up. Focused on the water, he mutters, "No time for that. I have to catch fish."

It sounds like a joke. But it's the reality for many people, every single day. No time for the essential, because we're too busy with the nonessential.

So, the real question is: what is essential?

For me, it all boils down to one thing, one simple, central question: "How can I get from where I am to where I want to be, with the least amount of effort, and in the shortest time possible?"

That's really all there is to it. You don't need to know anything more, because everything in life boils down to this: There is a **CURRENT** state, what IS right now. And there is a **TARGET** state, what we WANT instead; the vision we hold in our minds. That's it. And obviously, we don't want to reach that **TARGET** state slowly and with maximum effort. No, we want to get there as quickly and with as little effort as possible. Agreed?

Now, you might be thinking: "Typical economist, always looking for maximum gain with minimum effort. Where's the humanity in that?" Here's the answer: the same principle applies not only to money or measurable outcomes, but also to everything—even intangible values.

For a manager, a **TARGET** might be greater profitability.

For a Zen Buddhist, enlightenment.

For a government, lower unemployment.

For a mother, the well-being of her children is.

These aren't economic goals. They're human ones. And this is where the LO^2LA Principle comes in, as a universal tool to help you get there faster and with less resistance. It works in your private life, in business, in sports, in politics, in relationships, in society. It's about bridging the gap between where you are and where you want to be, with clarity and efficiency.

I have yet to meet a single person who truly wanted to reach their goals as slowly and painfully as possible.

And yet, this idea of achieving our goals with as little effort as possible runs directly counter to much of our Western-Christian upbringing. We are taught that life is supposed to be hard. That only through sweat, struggle, and sacrifice can we earn our bread and our worth. The more we toil, the more we supposedly deserve. Even Eastern wisdom sometimes echoes this belief.

I once read a book on management and Zen that said something like, "Don't be fooled, real effort is always required."

Its message was clear: only those who put in the work get the reward. But the LO²LA Principle suggests the opposite:

You don't need to struggle. You don't need to force. There is a faster, simpler, and more elegant way to solve problems and reach your goals. It might put me at odds with long-standing philosophies, but I feel I'm in good company. One of the greatest wisdom teachers of all time, Jesus, taught: "Look at the birds of the air! They neither sow nor reap nor gather into barns, and yet your heavenly Father feeds them. Are you not worth much more than they? Consider the lilies of the field, how they grow! They neither toil nor spin; yet I tell you that even Solomon in all his glory was not clothed like one of these" (Matthew 6:26).

This message is not one of exhaustion, but one of trust and alignment. And it's deeply economical. You'll be hard-pressed to find a more radical statement about human effort and abundance.

Yet, oddly enough, our culture and education system have absorbed almost none of this. Instead, we glorify the ideal of the tireless worker, the one who earns success through sheer effort. Now, let me be clear: I'm not advocating laziness. I'm advocating a better way—a more efficient, natural, and life-aligned way. That brings me to an essential point about goals: The LO^2LA Principle doesn't prescribe how to achieve specific goals or judge them as good or bad. That would be a human value judgment, and this principle goes deeper than that. What I'm offering is not a list of goals to pursue, but a universal mechanism, principles of life that apply to any goal.

These are not my laws. They aren't man-made. They have always been this way. They are now. And they always will be.

If we understand these laws, we can work with them, saving ourselves time, energy, and unnecessary suffering. If we don't understand them, we risk working against them, often without even realizing it, making our lives harder than they have to be. I know this from personal experience. For half my life, I struggled needlessly, until I reached a breaking point and thought, "This can't be it. There has to be another way." That search, and the answers it revealed, gave birth to what I now call "The LO^2LA Principle."

Part One: The Human Drama

"We find consolations, we find anesthetics, we learn skills with which we deceive ourselves. But we do not find the essential, the way of the ways."
—Hermann Hesse, Siddhartha

1. Expulsion From Paradise

"It is not for me to judge another person's life!"
—Hermann Hesse, Siddhartha

One of the core challenges we carry as human beings is our constant tendency to judge, labeling things as either good or bad. We judge ourselves, other people, and nearly every situation we encounter. But here's the catch: what's good for one person may be bad for another. What benefits the farmer might harm the miller down the road. And just like that, conflict is set in motion. This division between good and bad isn't based on any universal law of nature; it's a human construct. Moral standards shift over time and vary from culture to culture, even from one community to the next. The only constant is this: judgment breeds conflict. Conflict within us, and conflict between us. And when taken far enough, it even becomes the seed of war.

So where does this habit of judging, of dividing the world into good and evil, come from? Many of us were introduced to it early on, in one of the oldest stories ever told: the tale of Adam and Eve. According to the story, they ate from the Tree of the Knowledge of Good and Evil. And here's the striking part: before that moment, there was no mention of "good" or "evil." The story itself suggests that these judgments weren't part of our original nature. What existed before that division? A different kind of state, one where there was no labeling, no moral sorting. And that state had a name: paradise. But paradise, as it turns out, isn't a distant land or some future reward. It's a mindset. A way of being. A state of non-judgment, where we stop labeling ourselves, others, and the world around us as either right or wrong, good or bad.

Every one of us can return to that state. No one is keeping us from it, except ourselves. The story doesn't say that Adam and Eve were thrown out of paradise against their will. They made a choice. By choosing judgment, they stepped out. And that's precisely why we can step back in by choosing non-judgment. The door to paradise is still open. It always has been.

Here's something we should keep firmly in mind:

Our problems began the moment we started dividing the world into "good" and "evil."

It may sound bold, but think about it for a moment. If you didn't judge yourself, others, or situations, how many of your problems would remain? That's not just a rhetorical question. It's an invitation to pause and reflect.

Judgment is not a law of nature; it's a human habit. Nature, in all its wisdom, doesn't label or condemn. It simply is.

Imagine if the sun took a moral stance: *Mr. Smith committed a crime, no sunlight for him today. Mrs. Jones donated to a good cause; she gets extra warmth.* Absurd, right? The world would quickly descend into chaos. And yet, this is precisely the kind of discord we create among ourselves every day, through our constant judging. If nature were like us, life on Earth would be unpredictable and unfair. Thankfully, the sun shines on everyone equally. The river doesn't refuse to flow for one person over another. Nature operates beyond judgment. And maybe, just maybe, that's a hint at how we could live, too.

Let's take a lesson from nature. Let's be grateful that at least one force in our life remains free of judgment and consider what our world might look like if we followed suit.

Incidentally, this is also reflected in the Bible: "For He maketh His sun to rise on the evil and on the good, and sendeth rain on the just and on the unjust" (Matthew 5:45).

It's only human beings who cling so tightly to judgment, as if it were a virtue in and of itself. I see this time and again in my seminars: people holding on to their judgments like treasured trophies. And honestly, it's understandable. Because if we were to give up judging, we'd also have to give up something many people quietly enjoy—the ability to look down on others. Without judgment, you can't label your neighbor, your coworker, or a stranger as wrong, foolish, or bad. Pointing the finger and calling someone out as "evil" or "wrong" creates an illusion of superiority. It can feel good. Reassuring, even. However, here's the catch: that same act of judgment is what fuels our conflicts, stress, and division.

If we genuinely want to solve our problems, whether in our personal lives, workplaces, or society at large, we must be willing to let go of judgment. Without that shift, peace will remain out of reach. Harmony will stay theoretical. If we choose to believe that the world is composed of good people and bad people, then we also accept the inevitable tensions and struggles that accompany this belief. And if we try to build a more peaceful world while still clinging to judgment, we're setting ourselves up for failure.

What does this mean for you, personally? It means that a more harmonious, fulfilling life will only be possible when you stop dividing people, including yourself, into good and bad. Judgment is the seed of conflict. Release it, and you begin to create space for peace.

Even well-meaning institutions, such as religious organizations, the United Nations, and various ethical associations, often struggle to create lasting peace. It's not due to a lack of effort or intention. The problem lies deeper: these institutions, like many of us, continue to operate from a framework that divides the world into good and evil. And when you judge, even in the name of virtue, you reinforce the very division you aim to overcome. The Swiss psychologist Carl Jung once put it bluntly: "Virtue is more dangerous to man than vice." Why? Because a virtuous person, convinced of their moral high ground, is often quicker to condemn. That condemnation, no matter how noble its motive, breeds new conflict, precisely the opposite of what was intended.

It can be hard to accept this. We're conditioned to believe that fighting for "the good" will lead to peace. However, history and our own experience tell a different story. Take, for example, one of the most prolonged and painful conflicts in modern history: the relationship between Israel and the Palestinians. Decades of mutual condemnation, of labeling the other side as "evil," have led to suffering on a massive scale, many lives lost, entire communities devastated, and economies drained. And yet, for all the blood and billions spent, meaningful progress has been elusive. There was a temporary peace once, as some of you may recall. An offering of an open hand instead of a clenched fist. A small gesture. A change in attitude. This wasn't achieved with grand strategies or vast resources, but with a shift in mindset. A shift away from judgment and toward understanding. That's the power of dropping the labels, of letting go of good and evil as fixed categories. It opens space for movement. For healing. For genuine solutions that judgment alone could never bring about.

And yet, something strange continues to happen. There are still leaders, groups, and individuals who cling tightly to condemnation. They choose conflict over resolution. That's their right, of course. But let's be honest: if someone actively chooses conflict, they can't reasonably complain about the suffering that follows. We reap what we sow.

What's even more striking, though, is what isn't happening. Even after seeing powerful examples demonstrating what's possible when judgment is set aside, we seem unable to apply those lessons elsewhere. We don't use them to resolve conflicts in our companies, in our communities, or even within our own families.

That's what I meant when I referenced aliens in the introduction. Imagine a being from another world visiting Earth once every thousand years. From a scientific or technological perspective, they'd be impressed: we've mapped the genome, landed on the moon, and confirmed that the Earth revolves around the sun. But from a human or moral standpoint, would they see much progress? Probably not. The core problems—division, judgment, and conflict—remain unchanged. Technological advancement hasn't led to greater wisdom or compassion. The moon landing, for all its wonder, hasn't resolved our social or ethnic conflicts. It hasn't eased poverty or helped the unemployed find meaning and purpose.

And history is full of stories of reconciliation and healing that show what's possible when we stop dividing the world into good and evil (if you've never read about the 1914 Christmas Truce, please do). But we don't need to consult history books to understand this. Most of us have lived it.

Think about your own life. How many times have you quickly judged something as "bad," only to realize, years later, that it wasn't so bad after all? Maybe it even led to unexpected growth or opportunity. Perhaps it had a hidden purpose. But in that first moment of condemnation, conflict is born. From an economic standpoint, conflict is always costly, wasting time, energy, and resources. This is the price we pay for judgment. And it's one we keep paying, even when the returns are clearly negative.

If we insist on dividing the world into good and evil, then we should be honest with ourselves: we don't have the right to be surprised, or upset, by the personal and global problems that come with it. If there's anything truly worth being concerned about, it's not the world "out there." It's our own persistent inability to move beyond this duality. That's the real issue.

No one forced us out of paradise. We left it ourselves. We chose judgment. And yet, this is the hopeful part: paradise hasn't disappeared. It's still here. But don't wait for others to take you there; you may wait forever.

This isn't about the world. It's not even about society. It's about you. Paradise is just a thought away, but it's a thought only you can think. No one else can do it for you.

We'll revisit this theme throughout the book, because it lies at the heart of everything. This is the core human dilemma. The line that separates paradise from suffering isn't drawn by fate or circumstance; our own judgments draw it. And the moment we stop dividing, we begin returning.

2. How to Turn Yourself into a Powerless Person

"Too much knowledge had hindered him, too many holy verses, too many sacrificial rules, too much mortification, too much doing and striving!"
—Hermann Hesse, Siddhartha

Human beings possess immense power, so immense, in fact, that we even have the power to give it away. And we do so, often and enthusiastically. It almost seems like one of humanity's favorite habits: surrendering our own strength and declaring ourselves powerless. In my seminars, I regularly witness how fiercely people cling to this illusion. Some even argue passionately for their own helplessness. Nothing unsettles some individuals more than hearing the simple truth: You are powerful. Because with power comes something many would rather avoid: responsibility. And responsibility, for some, is a step too far. It's far easier to identify as the victim. Victims are not required to act. They can blame, complain, and defer to others. It's a familiar and comfortable role for many.

If you feel resistance rising at this idea, that's okay. This book may not be for you right now. Maybe in a few years, you'll come back to it with different eyes.

In the chapters ahead, we'll explore the clever ways we disempower ourselves and how we can stop.

2.1 Fear

Fear touches nearly every aspect of our lives. It can be the fear of getting sick, losing a job, facing a recession, being judged, or fearing your boss or coworkers. Then there's the fear of taking responsibility, the fear of criticism, and the fear of violence or conflict. The list could go on forever.

To manage this constant undercurrent of fear, society has developed two major systems: insurance and the welfare state. Add to that the ever-growing spending on national defense. Together, they offer a degree of material safety, serving as a buffer against uncertainty. Just think about the size of these industries and the amount of money tied up in them. That alone gives us a clue about the depth of our collective anxiety. In a material world, it makes sense to buy a sense of security.

But here's the more profound truth: the real problem isn't external. It's internal. Fear stems from insecurity. Insecurity breeds anxiety, and anxiety triggers defense, aggression, and struggle. The more insecure we feel, the more fearful we become, and the more reactive, controlling, and even hostile we may be.

Insecurity, at its core, is a lack of trust. A lack of trust in ourselves. A lack of trust in others. A lack of trust in life.

Now, let's consider something interesting. Most people around the world identify with some religion. They believe in a higher power, often a God described as all-knowing, all-powerful, and ever-present. And yet, those same people frequently feel the need to buy insurance and build elaborate safety nets. That behavior sends an unmistakable message: *Trust in God is good, but have a safety net just in case.*

There's nothing wrong with insurance. If you lack trust in life, it's logical to protect yourself. But what does it say about our collective mindset? Despite our religious affiliations, we function mainly as a godless society, not in a moral or judgmental sense, but in the sense that our trust in life, in the universe, in whatever you choose to call it, is fundamentally weak.

And this lack of trust has consequences.

Fear makes us cling to ideas, dogmas, belief systems, relationships, and careers. We hold on tightly because we think it gives us stability, identity, and safety. But here's the irony: the more tightly we hold on, the more we block our own growth. What we cling to becomes stagnant. And what cannot move dies. This isn't abstract philosophy; it's real life. I once spoke with a client who shared the story of an employee who died of cancer within six months. That man was known for holding on, rigidly, to everything: control, routines, grievances. His body mirrored that inner rigidity.

Some even claim that fear is helpful, that it protects us. That belief, however widespread, is deeply flawed. Think about it: if fear really protected us, then the more afraid we were, the safer we'd be. But the opposite is true. Fear attracts exactly what we're afraid of. Trust, not fear, is what truly protects us.

Where's the logic in this? Where's the common sense?

This may sound counterintuitive, but it's echoed across spiritual traditions. The Bible teaches that fear invites the very thing we dread. The poet and philosopher Muhammad Iqbal, a spiritual leader to millions, wrote, "Despair is poison to life… Powerlessness is the fruit of despair. O, you, prisoner of your worries, learn from the Prophet the message 'Do not worry'." And what's even more concrete in the context of the LO^{2}LA Principle, "Fear robs the foot of the power to move forward, and it robs your intellect of the ability to think."

The principles that make up the LO^{2}LA Principle aren't simply poetic ideas; they're practical truths observable in sports. In curling, a stone thrown hesitantly and fearfully is called a "fear stone." Unsurprisingly, it never goes where the player truly intended. Even the smallest dose of fear disrupts the natural rhythm of life. That's true in sports, at work, in relationships, even in politics.

Let's sum it up: Fear is born from a lack of trust in life. It triggers defensive behaviors and blocks both the flow of life and our ability to think clearly. It drains energy and clouds judgment.

Fear will never help you solve problems or reach your goals. Trust will.

2.2 Sin

The concept of sin plays a surprisingly practical role in discussions of powerlessness. Far from being just a spiritual concern, sin has been used for centuries, millennia, really, as a tool for control.

The mechanism is simple and, unfortunately, very effective:

First, people are told they're inherently flawed. "You are all sinners," the message goes. That idea creates guilt. And guilt, as any parent, leader, or marketer knows, makes people easier to manipulate. This works just as well with grown-ups as it does with children. Once someone feels guilty, they're more likely to comply, to give in, to surrender their power. But here's where it gets clever: you don't just leave people drowning in guilt. That would seem cruel. No, you offer them a solution. You offer redemption. Salvation. A way out. All they have to do is follow certain rules, obey certain authorities, or, sometimes, make a payment. And just like that, the burden of sin is lifted. But not entirely.

Because if people felt too safe, they might stop obeying. So, the guilt can't disappear completely. The idea of sin has to remain hanging over their heads like a cloud, a constant reminder of their unworthiness. That's what keeps them in check.

You may have heard it said like this: A 'chosen' man (chosen by whom?) stands before a crowd and declares with gravity, "You are all sinners. Come to me, while there's still time. I'll show you the way to salvation."

This formula works. It's powerful. Which makes it all the more puzzling: Why do we let it work on us? Why do people keep giving away their power to others, especially those who claim the authority to judge right and wrong, guilt and innocence? Think about it. Where does one person get the right to judge another? Where does any institution get the authority to decide what counts as a sin?

Sin is not a law of nature. It's not like gravity or death. It's a human invention, one that has been used skillfully to dominate, shame, and subdue. As long as someone submits to this framework, they remain stuck. They cannot step into their own strength.

Now, this isn't about attacking spiritual teachers or religious leaders. And it's certainly not about condemning faith itself. Ultimately, the responsibility lies with each individual. No one is forcing anyone to give up their power. People do it willingly, sometimes even gratefully.

Still, it's hard to understand why so many continue to hand over that power, especially within traditions that are supposed to set people free. I once read a sentence in a Christian magazine that struck me: "We need both, the Messiah who comes as judge of the nations, and people who are willing to submit to a new ethic."

Wait, what? The Messiah as judge of nations?

Let's pause for a moment and really consider that. If all nations are assumed to be sinful, then judgment becomes the next logical step. But what exactly is the purpose of judging entire nations? Which nation will be judged more, which less? Who decides which is better or worse? And does the act of judgment actually improve anything?

The logic doesn't hold up. Jesus himself challenged it. Over two thousand years ago, he said something that still rings true: "Judge not, lest you be judged." And what do we do, again and again? We judge others.

As soon as we label someone a sinner, we're judging them. And in doing so, we go directly against what Jesus himself taught. Yet many of us still call ourselves Christians.

It's difficult to understand why so many people are willing to make themselves powerless by accepting the label of sinner. And yet, we see the consequences of this mindset everywhere: constant accusations, tension, conflict, even war. And above all, a growing inability to solve the challenges we face.

There's a powerful tale from the East that shows how a strong, free being can be turned into something weak and dependent.

The Sheep and the Lions

A flock of sheep was peacefully grazing in a meadow when, suddenly, lions appeared from the forest and attacked. Blood was spilled. Chaos followed. The lions stayed and took away the sheep's freedom. The sheep suffered greatly under the superior power of the lions.

Eventually, the sheep came together to discuss what could be done. It was clear things couldn't go on like this. Among them was an old and clever sheep who said:

"We can't defeat the lions by force. We can't become lions ourselves. But maybe, just maybe, we can make the lions forget who they are. Maybe we can turn wild lions into tame sheep."

The others agreed to try.

The clever sheep began to preach to the lions: "O, you arrogant creatures! You who know nothing of eternal punishment! I come to you as a messenger of God. I am bringing you the truth. You must abandon your savage ways. Righteous beings do not feed on meat; they eat grass. God loves the meek. Your sharp teeth are a shameful reminder of your violence. True paradise belongs to the weak and humble. Wealth is a temptation; poverty is a virtue. If you seek favor with God, stop killing sheep; kill your own instincts instead! Close your eyes, your ears, your mouths. This pasture is nothing but an illusion. Don't cling to illusions!" And so, it happened.

The lions, tired of conflict and intrigued by this message of peace, began to change. Slowly, they adopted the sheep's religion. They started to eat grass. Their teeth grew dull. The fierce light in their eyes faded. Their courage weakened. They lost their power, their pride, and eventually even their health. They began to fear death, fear judgment, fear everything. Fear brought diseases they had never known. Poverty and small-mindedness infiltrated what was once a proud and strong group.

The sheep had succeeded in putting the lions to sleep. The lions called this new state "Moral Culture."

The Lesson? If you can convince someone that they are sinful and keep them afraid, you can turn them into a weak and dependent person. And from there, they're easy to control.

In fact, if you're thinking of forming a sect, this is a recipe that has worked for thousands of years and continues to do so.

But let's look at it from a different, more uplifting angle: Don't let anyone tell you that you're a sinner. Instead, ask yourself: "Why would someone want to make me feel powerless? What motive might they have for keeping me in fear and guilt?" And ask yourself this, too: "How does the idea of sin fit within a worldview based on Christian love?" It doesn't. Unconditional love doesn't divide the world up into good and bad.

2.3 Shifting Blame

Shifting blame is one of the most common social habits and one of the most subtle ways we give away our power. We've all heard the usual lines: "It's Jack's fault." "The government messed it up." "It's the recession." "My boss is the problem."

On the surface, these sound like harmless complaints. But let's take a closer look.

First, notice the language. The word "fault" often carries the same weight as "guilt", and guilt has its roots in the idea of sin. In other words, when we assign blame, we're not just stating facts; we're judging. We're casting someone else as the wrongdoer—the sinner. And we, by contrast, have judged them.

Secondly, and that's at the heart of it: whenever we shift blame, we're also shifting power to someone else. If I'm not responsible, then I'm not in control. If I'm not in control, then I'm dependent on others. That means I'm powerless, and someone else is powerful. It's the classic victim-perpetrator dynamic. The media thrives on stories of victims. And the victim role is, in many ways, socially rewarded. People who carry the title of "victim" often get sympathy, support, attention, and even admiration, especially if they bear their suffering "bravely."

But here's what's often overlooked: Being a victim means being powerless. Is that really what it means to be human? Are we designed to live at the mercy of outside forces, with no say in how life unfolds? If that were true, human existence would seem unbearably limited, if not downright unacceptable.

What's even more disturbing is how fiercely people cling to their powerlessness. In some cases, they become aggressive about defending it. It's as if being a victim gives their life meaning. Some even want to be victims of other people, of accidents, of illnesses. It's medieval thinking in the middle of a technologically advanced civilization.

Let's look at how this plays out in everyday life.

The Sales Manager

Imagine a sales manager who's worked for the same company for seven years. Business has been tough, but he's kept his job and feels confident he'll stay on. He sees this as a result of his competence, and he's proud of it. He's taking responsibility for his success. So far, so good.

But then, unexpectedly, he's let go. And immediately, the story changes. Suddenly, it's not about his performance anymore. Now it's his manager's fault. Or the recession. Or the client who didn't come through with the big order. The responsibility is quickly transferred to someone or something else.

This is our default mental habit: When things go well, we take credit. When they don't, we find someone to blame.

The same thing happens when we drive a car. If we get to our destination safely, we say we're skilled drivers. However, if an accident occurs, then the weather, the other driver, or the road conditions are often blamed. We assign responsibility according to convenience, not consistency.

At one point, it even became fashionable to blame one's childhood. Someone would commit a crime, even murder, and explain it by saying, "I had a difficult upbringing." And, of course, the parents could then point to their own childhoods, and so the chain of blame continues endlessly.

But where does that lead us? Nowhere.

We've become experts at inventing excuses and finding scapegoats. We've even built entire fields of study, libraries full of books, and whole social systems around that. But the price we pay is high: the more we blame, the more we weaken ourselves.

As long as we hold on to the victim mindset, we are turning ourselves into powerless beings. We rob ourselves of the one thing that could actually change our lives: responsibility.

In truth, we are never the victim of other people, institutions, or events. We are always, first and foremost, the victim of our own thinking.

And here's the paradox: our power is so great that we can actually use it to make ourselves powerless, if we choose to. And for reasons that are hard to explain, many people do precisely that.

2.4 The Urge to Interfere

Many people feel a strong, almost irresistible urge to interfere in the lives of others. They jump at the chance to point out what someone has done wrong or what they should be doing differently. But of course, it's never framed as interference; it's always done in the name of virtue. After all, you're not being unkind. You're just trying to help. You know better. Right?

But let's pause here and ask: What does "better" actually mean? And who decides what's better for someone else?

Well, the so-called good guys usually decide. And who are the good guys? Conveniently, they decide that, too. But what happens when the bad guys also claim to be the good guys? That's not hypothetical; it happens all the time, especially in politics. So now what?

Now we're in the middle of a full-blown conflict. Because interference almost always involves judgment. And judgment almost always leads to conflict. The truth is, people who carry unresolved conflicts within themselves feel compelled to solve disputes in others by "helping" them. It has never worked before, and it won't work a thousand years from now.

Even large-scale, well-meaning efforts, such as those of the United Nations, fail. Despite its mission to promote peace, its interventions haven't reduced the number of conflicts worldwide. In fact, for every conflict that seems to calm down, two new ones often arise. The UN tries to intervene everywhere, but at best, it offers surface-level solutions and temporary relief. It looks good on paper, you can feel like you've "done something," and go to sleep at night feeling responsible. However, the reality is that the deeper issues persist and continue to multiply.

Religion shows a similar pattern. Christians might feel fortunate that religions like Islam and Buddhism usually don't put much energy into converting others. But when that restraint disappears, things can turn ugly; just look at Islamic fundamentalism for a glimpse of how far interference can go. The irony, of course, is that Christianity has a long history of doing exactly what it fears: interfering, converting, and "correcting" others. The West may fear extremism, but it's been practicing its own brand of it for centuries.

But we don't need to look at the global stage to understand the problem. Just look around you.

How often do we interfere in the lives of the people closest to us?

Mrs. Miller has no idea how to raise her kids.

Mr. Myers doesn't mow his lawn often enough.

If Ken keeps this up, he's going to lose his job.

Mrs. Smith's lifestyle is bound to blow up in her face.

We tell ourselves, "We know how to do it. They don't." The only problem? They're thinking the same thing about us.

That's mutual interference. And it keeps us stuck in conflict. Round and round we go. Humanity has been running this loop for generations.

Now, there's another layer to this, one we won't fully explore here: There are always people and systems that benefit from conflict. And if someone profits from conflict, then peace is not in their interest.

2.5 The Search Outside Ourselves

"When someone is searching, it easily happens that his eye only sees the thing he is looking for, that he is unable to find anything, to let anything into himself, because he only ever thinks of what he is looking for, because he has a goal, because he is obsessed with the goal. To seek means to have a goal. But to find means to be free, to be open, to have no goal. You, venerable one, are often indeed a seeker, because, striving for your goal, you do not see many things that are close before your eyes."

—Hermann Hesse, Siddhartha

We've become accustomed to looking outward for help, answers, and solutions to our problems. This tendency is another clear sign that we don't trust our own inner power or wisdom. Every time we do this, we're handing our power over to someone or something else.

But why do we seek answers outside ourselves? Because we believe there's nothing within. And that reveals a deeper issue: many people simply don't value their inner world.

So, where exactly do we turn for guidance?

To experts, doctors, psychologists, lawyers, astrologers, graphologists, clairvoyants, and so on. We expect others to think for us, to fix our problems, to decide our direction. This is dangerous because it means we're delegating the most essential task of all: thinking. They become everything, and we become nothing.

This dynamic is evident in the crowds of people who travel to gurus in India, Tibet, or Japan. These seekers trust others to do what they don't trust themselves to do. And that's precisely what stunts their growth. Every movement is directed away from the individual's own center.

Now, let's be clear: turning to outside guidance isn't always wrong. Sometimes, it's necessary and even wise. But we should be conscious of what we're doing. When we place authority in someone else's hands, we're giving away our own. And it's worth asking: "Will this actually solve the problem?"

Several examples illustrate how this plays out in real life.

When the Stars Decide

A young woman once visited an astrologer. She was uncertain about her future and didn't know which direction to take. The astrologer told her, "Things will get better after September 15."

That single statement turned her into a powerless figure. Before September 15, she believed she could do nothing because she thought things would be difficult. And after September 15, she believed she didn't need to do anything because things would improve on their own.

In both cases, she gave away her agency. She stopped being a human being and became a puppet of the stars.

The Man who Gave Away his Heart

A middle-aged man had to undergo a heart transplant. Complications followed, and for three years, he bounced from specialist to specialist. He could no longer work, and he devoted all his energy to studying his illness and trying every therapy he could find. Yet nothing helped.

Eventually, his heart specialist told him honestly, "There's nothing more we can do. Now it's up to you. You have to find your inner strength."

But he didn't. He couldn't.

He had given all his power to doctors, treatments, and the medical system. He clung to the belief that someone else had to fix him. The idea that he had the power to change his life terrified him more than the idea of dying.

When I last saw him, he said, "If this goes on, I'll probably die." I congratulated him on the insight and reminded him that dying was, of course, his right. But I also told him: "You don't have to die. You just have to wake up to your own power."

He didn't want that. Waking up would mean taking action. It would mean taking responsibility. And that meant giving up the comforting idea that he was a victim of fate.

Other people cannot solve our problems. Period. Even on the national level, we see how outside help often backfires. Development aid to Africa is a striking example. While intended to help, much of it has actually slowed down progress. Many Africans have recognized this them-selves: that foreign aid has caused more damage than benefit. Waiting for help from outside breeds a sense of helplessness.

In short, once again, we use our power to give away our power.

And this tendency runs deep. I once read a line in a magazine that stopped me cold:

"Even today, the world is still waiting for the one who will establish peace on earth, the Messiah. And it also waits for a new heart, a new way of thinking, which can only come through the Spirit of God."

How convenient. All we need to do is wait. And in the meantime? We fight wars, cause harm, and tell ourselves that the "new thinking" hasn't arrived yet because the

Spirit of God hasn't shown up. But can anyone honestly believe this is how progress happens?

This kind of thinking hides two significant forms of powerlessness:

1. The responsibility for peace is shifted to someone else.

2. Help is expected from outside.

So again, we wait. And nothing changes.

And here's the question that truly troubles me: If peace and a new way of thinking can only come from God, then what exactly is God waiting for? Haven't there been enough wars? Enough suffering? Why the delay? Or maybe this is a classic feedback loop, something known in computer science: we're waiting for God, and God is waiting for us.

Result? The system stalls. Nothing happens.
It will stay this way until someone, anyone, decides to stop waiting. My advice is simple: stop waiting for help to come from the outside.

Let me share another quote from Islamic philosopher Mohammad Iqbal, who expressed this mindset with striking clarity: "God loves the person who deserves his life. Misfortune on the one who feeds from another's table; he has sold his honor for a coin. Blessed is the man, thirsting under the sun, who does not ask for a cup of water. His forehead is not wet with the shame of begging; he is still a man, not a piece of clay. This honorable young man walks with his head held high like a tree. Are his hands empty?

He is all the more master of himself. An entire ocean, obtained by begging, is nothing but a sea of fire."

Now, I am not advocating for Islam. But could this message of inner strength be part of the reason why some in the West fear it? In our comfortable social welfare system, we've traded strength for servitude. We've become dependent on too many institutions, on systems, structures, services, and saviors. And that will never, ever be the way to solve our problems truly. Not for a nation. And not for an individual.

2.6 The Complexity of Life

I'm firmly convinced, and I'll do my best to show this, that the truth is simple. It has to be. Because if the truth were complicated, it would only be accessible to a tiny elite of people with above-average intelligence. And that simply doesn't make sense.

Yet, in our everyday reality, nearly everything is made to seem incredibly complex. That complexity serves a purpose: it benefits the experts. The more complicated something appears, the more justification there is to elevate those who "understand it", to pay them more, revere them more, and depend on them more. Strangely, some people only feel convinced by something once they don't understand it. And others become less convinced the moment they do understand it. That may sound absurd, but it's something I encounter regularly in my workshops. Every so often, someone will exclaim: "No, it can't be that simple!"

But that reaction reveals something more profound. It's not really about logic; it's about power. Because if something is simple, that means anyone can use it, including you. And that means you'd have to act on it. You'd have to change something in your own life.

But if it's complicated? Well then, you've got an excuse: "It's too hard." "It takes too much time." "No one else can do it either."

And so, we protect ourselves from change. Not because the truth is too complex, but because it's too accessible.

Even research in chaos theory, the study of seemingly random systems, has confirmed this: the most complex patterns are built from incredibly simple rules. The deeper we look into nature, behavior, or life, the simpler things become. However, when we skim the surface and analyze everything through scientific or intellectual frameworks, we inevitably make it more complicated.

Take walking, for example. It's simple. Nearly everyone can do it. But if we tried to describe walking in complete detail, analyzing every muscle movement and every balance shift, we'd fill entire libraries. And still, it's unlikely anyone could learn to walk just by reading those books.

Walking is simple when practiced, and nearly impossible when over-analyzed.

This example may not have serious consequences. But when the same thing happens with something like love, the impact is much greater. We can, and often do, philosophize endlessly about love. We define it, debate it, dissect it. The result? Most people no longer know what love is. And more importantly, they don't practice it.

Practicing love is simple. But analyzing love? That's complicated. So complicated that there's no time or energy left to do it.

Sometimes in my seminars, I'll explain that every human problem can be resolved through love. And instantly, a wave of ifs, buts, and objections fills the room. The conversation becomes increasingly complex. And that complexity offers the perfect justification: "This is obviously not as simple as it sounds." And so, we don't have to do anything.

Simplicity as Truth

Balthasar Staehelin, a respected Swiss physician and psychologist, wrote something in the early 1970s that still rings true today. In his book, *Die Welt als Du (The World as You)*, he observed: "In today's medicine and psychology, we are missing both the true and the simple."

And we can see the consequences everywhere, especially in healthcare.

In most developed countries, healthcare systems have become so complex, fragmented, and bureaucratic that they are no longer financially sustainable. Costs have skyrocketed, outcomes are often mediocre, and yet the system continues to grow more complicated every year. A while ago, I heard an expert on French radio speaking about the cost explosion in healthcare. He mentioned that three ultrasound scans are more than enough during pregnancy.

But it made me think: *How did babies get delivered safely before ultrasound machines even existed? And how do millions of children continue to be born in places with far less access to 'advanced' prenatal care?*

Some people point to our medical technology as a sign of progress. But I see it more as a symptom of confusion. When we rely too heavily on external complexity, we lose touch with internal clarity.

Don't just talk, do.

Like Balthasar Staehelin, I believe that truth is not only powerful but also simple. In fact, it must be simple. And if it's not simple, it's probably not true.

Rather than talk endlessly about what could be done, or debate the nuances until we're exhausted, we'd be better off just doing the thing.

Because the truth is always simple, and anyone who insists on making simple things complicated isn't helping. They're only standing in the way of their own growth.

2.7 Reason and Analysis

For much of modern science and management, reason and analysis have been treated as the gold standard, the key tools for understanding the world and solving problems. But today, that assumption is being increasingly questioned. There's a growing awareness that relying solely on intellect and logic may not actually lead us to the deepest insights or the best solutions.

I don't need to dwell too long on this point; there's plenty of literature on the topic. What matters here is this: When we rely only on reason, we drastically limit our potential.

Reason, by nature, can only work with the information it already has. It's bound to the past and the present; it knows nothing about the future. And even in the present, it only sees a tiny sliver of what's really happening. That's a weak foundation on which to build decisions. And yet, for generations, we've placed enormous trust in the rational mind. But if you really think about it, it's hard to understand why reason has been held in such high regard for so long. When you make decisions based only on logic, the odds of making a wrong call are actually very high. And on the flip side, truly extraordinary success seldom comes from pure analysis. Take a look at history; virtually none of the world's breakthrough products or businesses were created solely from rational calculations of market needs.

One of the clearest examples of this is the infamous Ford Edsel. In the 1950s, Ford conducted what may have been the most extensive market research ever done for a car. They wanted to design a vehicle that perfectly fit public demand. On paper, everything made sense. In reality, the Edsel turned out to be one of the biggest flops in automotive history, costing Ford hundreds of millions of dollars.

Why? Because the Edsel was too rational. Too average. Too calculated. Nobody wanted it.

Now compare that to Ray Kroc, the man behind McDonald's. In 1960, he defied the advice of his lawyers and purchased the rights to the McDonald's name. He didn't have market data or focus groups telling him to do it; he had a gut feeling.

And the rest is history. You can't plan that kind of vision with charts and spreadsheets.

The lesson is clear: great success rarely starts with logic alone. Reason always looks outside, to the world, to data, to analysis. And while that's not useless, it's also not enough. The more profound truth—the kind that changes lives—comes from within. The more someone clings to reason, the less they tend to trust themselves. They put more faith in external analysis than in their own intuition, experience, or internal compass. This book has already touched on this idea. In Chapter 2.5, I talked about how we tend to search for answers "out there," rather than turning inward. Well, "reason" is exactly that: an outward search. And those who rely only on it are often the most insecure, because they've placed all their power in tools that can't see the whole picture.

Even science proves its own limitations. Theories based on logic are constantly being replaced. What we know today will seem outdated tomorrow. In contrast, the insights of spiritual teachers such as Jesus, the Buddha, and Laozi have endured for thousands of years. Why? Because they didn't rely on cold rationality. Their truths came from a deeper place.

Interestingly, even science itself is starting to recognize this. French biologist Joël de Rosnay, in his book *The Macroscope*, argued that traditional scientific methods actually distort reality rather than reveal it. Analytical thinking, he writes, isolates knowledge. It breaks things apart rather than showing how they're connected. The result? Narrow perspectives and rigid thinking.

This is a critical insight: reason and analysis restrict us. They put limits on human potential. That's why, throughout this book, I'll place a stronger emphasis on

analogical thinking, on comparing, connecting, and intuitively understanding the world. It opens up possibilities
that analysis alone can't reach.

Nowhere is the failure of pure reason more evident
than in the field of medicine.

In the last 150 years, many groundbreaking medical
discoveries were initially dismissed as unscientific, often by
university professors and scientific authorities. Their
reason told them it couldn't be true. One tragic example is
Dr. Louis Pillemer, the immunologist who discovered
Properdin, a critical part of the human immune system.
For years, his findings were questioned by other scientists.
Praise for his discovery quickly turned to doubt and
criticism. Overwhelmed by the rejection, he took his own
life. Months after his death, the medical establishment
began to recognize his research.

Medicine, unfortunately, has one of the darkest
histories when it comes to rejecting dissent, and all in the
name of "reason" and "science." But behind that rejection
often lies something else entirely: power.

At the very least, common sense should remind us of
this:

Today's experts mock the experts of 500 years ago.
And 500 years from now, people will mock our experts just
the same. Galileo was condemned for saying the Earth
revolves around the sun. Now, even children know it's
true.

Let's be careful not to dismiss ideas simply because they don't fit the prevailing view.

Reason, when it becomes rigid and narrow, holds us back. It builds walls where we should be building bridges. It looks for answers "out there," when true wisdom lives within.

2.8 The Inability to Think Independently

We humans like to believe we're rational, logical beings. And we place a great deal of trust in our ability to think clearly. But in this section, I want to challenge that belief. Because the truth is, our logic often fails us. We frequently think and act in ways that are anything but logical. As we've already seen in earlier examples, even science, our supposed beacon of reason, only accepts what fits into the prevailing worldview of the time. That's not independent thinking; it is intellectual conformity. Anyone with a basic knowledge of history is aware of how drastically scientific "truths" can shift in just a few years.

History also reveals something even more troubling: we appear to be hardwired for conflict. Our history books are packed with wars, invasions, and armed struggles. But what did these conflicts really achieve? Where are the once-glorious Roman Empire, imperial Spain, or mighty England now? If we were truly logical, we would've found better ways to live together by now. And it's not as though those alternatives haven't been offered; philosophers, sages, and visionaries have been proposing them for thousands of years. Still, we seem unable, or unwilling, to adopt them.

In the 19th century, the prevailing scientific worldview emphasized struggle and survival. Many people, especially in business, still think this way. But we now know that what science once interpreted as "exploitation" was, in fact, symbiosis. Evolution is not a battleground; it's a network of mutual support. The idea that parasites and predators govern nature is simply false. Most life forms thrive in cooperative relationships and understand (except humans) that everything is connected and that the demise of one species or 'enemy' poses a threat to the entire system. The predator-prey dynamic is the exception, not the rule. Yet that's the model we've chosen to emulate, possibly because it stands out.

Take cancer, for example. It's perhaps the most "successful" parasite, and that's precisely the problem. It consumes its host until both the host and the cancer die. Many economic systems function the same way: feeding off what sustains them until there's nothing left. Perhaps politicians and CEOs need to be trained in comparative thinking. Unfortunately, we have spent centuries reinforcing our linear thinking that now limits us.

We rarely recognize that there's more than one kind of logic. We're so conditioned by Aristotelian logic, the logic of "either/or," that we can't even imagine a plural form of the word "logic." But there are other logical systems, many of which were explored thousands of years ago in Eastern philosophy and are now being rediscovered in modern theoretical physics.

There isn't only good or bad, right or wrong. There's also "both/and." German physicist and philosopher, Werner Heisenberg, urged humanity to move beyond "the one-dimensional logic that cuts the world into fragments with the knife of either-or and leaves us trying to rebuild the world from the dismembered pieces."

Letting go of this mindset is hard work. It requires independent thought, and that's uncomfortable. Throughout this book, I'll revisit the concept of 'both/and' logic. I know that some readers may resist it and have their fair share of issues with it.

Every one of us could find examples in our own lives, if we truly wanted to, that show what leads to conflict and what leads to peace. But since we were never taught to think independently, we mostly adopt the patterns and beliefs of our parents and environment. So even though we live in a high-tech society, our thought patterns haven't evolved much since the Stone Age. That's absurd. We've put enormous effort into developing machines and our manufacturing capabilities, but we've invested very little into developing our thinking. A while ago, the concept of "limits to growth" gained popularity. A great deal of thought has been given to the idea that material growth must eventually come to an end. And that's fair.

But what we are really talking about here is a different kind of growth, the inner growth of human beings. This is, without doubt, the largest growth market imaginable. On the one hand, because human development is still in its infancy. And on the other hand, because there are no limits to growth in the human realm.

Some scientists might immediately object and say, "But humans are limited beings!" That's true, but only in the sense that we have made ourselves limited. And if we have the power to limit ourselves, then logically we also have the power to surpass those limits.

Let me give you a few more examples that show just how little we often think logically or independently:

In my leadership workshops, I've met highly intelligent individuals who start laughing or squirming when I talk about love. And yet, many of these same people are baptized Christians, married in church, and familiar with the most basic Christian principle: "Love your neighbor as yourself." So how is it possible to be part of the Christian faith, mock the topic of love, ruthlessly battle your competitors, and even justify violence?

You can do all of this, of course, but not while honestly calling yourself a follower of Christian values. My point is to show how thoughtless intelligent people can be. We're born into institutions, or join them later, and then stop

thinking about whether we even agree with their principles.

Here's a thought experiment: imagine we start a new
organization with just one rule: We don't judge other
people. How many members would we get? Probably very
few. Most people would admit that they don't live that way
and therefore can't sign up. That would at least be logical.
But many of these same people are members of churches
that make the exact same demand. They just don't think
about it. Where's the logic in this?

Please note, I'm not telling anyone to leave their
church. I'm calling for honest, independent thought. If
you're a member of a church, it would be logical to at least
try to live by its teachings. If you don't care about those
teachings, it would be honest to step away. Anything else
is dishonest.

And now let me ask: "How can a society that's based
on this kind of widespread dishonesty and thoughtlessness
ever hope to solve its problems?"

How can a Christian magazine publish the headline,
"We need a Messiah who comes as judge," when Jesus
himself said, "Judge not." Where's our logic?

Positive Thinking

A company enrolled four employees in a workshop on
'Positive Thinking.' A day before it was scheduled to begin,
they were told they wouldn't be going after all. The
company pulled the plug because business wasn't great.

What does that logic say? When things are going well, we can afford to think positively. When things are bad, we can't. The irony? That's when positive thinking is needed most.

Mosquito Bites

Consider this one: a woman said she no longer gets bitten by mosquitoes because she learned how to protect herself. Her colleague, a smart woman, responded: "But mosquitoes need blood to live. I read that in a book. It's not nice to keep your blood from them. Maybe that's why God created humans." Where is the logic? And yet we're still puzzled about why we're struggling with so many problems.

Take unemployment. It's another great example of our inability to think clearly and independently. Repeatedly, the proposal is made to work fewer hours so that more people can share the same amount of work. But this idea ignores one basic truth: the amount of work is not fixed. Work is not something static; people create it. And it's not created by working less, but by thinking creatively. Our belief that work is limited and that working less is beneficial has actually caused less work to exist. Now we're complaining about unemployment. But in truth, we are reaping exactly what we've sown. The law is simple: treat work as something bad and limited, and you will get less of it.

Just think of the inventions of Thomas Edison or Henry Ford. They didn't eliminate jobs; they created millions of them. Or look at the Swiss watch industry: thanks to Swatch, not only were jobs saved, but new ones were created. What are companies focused on today? Cutting costs by eliminating jobs. Not because there's no work, but because there's a lack of creativity and flexibility.

The goal isn't to redistribute a fixed amount of work; it's to create new work. But that requires imagination. And that's apparently harder than cutting hours and budgets.

We urgently need individuals who can think for themselves, people who are willing to challenge dogma, question conventions, and explore new ideas. Thankfully, such people have always existed. Pythagoras once said the Earth was round. That was outrageous back then. Much later, two other men, Bill Gates and Paul Allen, said something equally outrageous: "A computer on every desk and in every home." They were mocked. But today, it's reality.

So, if you come across an "outrageous" idea in this book, I have one request: forget everything you've learned and think it through for yourself. Test it in your own life. Don't just argue about it. Practice it. Because without action, ideas are meaningless. Gates and Allen didn't just talk about personal computers. They built them. And the world changed.

Let me leave you with this quote by the French nuclear physicist J.E. Charon: "Contrary to popular opinion, I am deeply convinced that science makes the greatest progress when it denies the facts of experience."

And you, too, will make your greatest progress when you begin to question the conventional views you've accepted all your life—even just once.

3. The Consequence: Our Problems Are Unsolvable

If you make yourself powerless, you obviously can't expect to reach your goals quickly or solve your problems effectively. And yet, we all know people who have managed to do exactly that. As an extreme example, and extremes are often the best way to reveal how something works, I'd like to mention Jesus of Nazareth.

Let's take the list of traits we've discussed so far, the ones that keep us trapped in powerlessness. If we compare them to Jesus, here's what we find:

Jesus was not afraid. Jesus did not see himself as a sinner. Jesus did not shift responsibility onto others. Jesus did not meddle in other people's affairs. Jesus did not seek salvation in the outside world. Jesus presented life in radically simple terms. Jesus did not rely solely on reason or analysis. Jesus thought independently and with true logic. Jesus thought in analogies.

And we all know what he accomplished. His inner power was immense. Now, some people might object: "Sure, Jesus could do that. But I'm not Jesus." To those people, I offer two responses.

First, I encourage you to think more independently. Take another look at that list. There's nothing in it that any of us can't at least strive toward. These are not superhuman traits. They are human traits.

Second, I suggest you take a closer look at the Bible. Jesus is quoted as saying: "What I have done, you can also do."

And that's not a metaphor. It's a direct statement. If anyone would know what's possible for human beings, surely it would be the person who did those things.

But here we are, more than 2,000 years later, and most people still haven't taken that sentence to heart.

We can do what we want, as individuals, as a society, or as a species, but if we are not willing to free ourselves from these self-limiting behaviors, then meaningful progress will remain out of reach. And no, we don't need another intellectual debate about whether these behaviors are "really" harmful. We don't need more analysis or theory. This is about life, about practice. Either you act on it and see what happens, or you don't. If you don't, all the theorizing in the world won't help.

In the second part of this book, we'll take a closer look at a crucial distinction: our work is not to solve the world's problems. That kind of interference is part of the problem.

Our work is to solve our own problems. Until we truly understand that human development will remain stalled.

Let me reiterate another important point: we cannot solve complex problems using our conventional logic, which is based on "either/or." Scientists like Frederic Vester, among others, have demonstrated how linear, conventional thinking actually worsens the interlinked challenges we face today. This is especially heartbreaking in medicine: look at the way we've approached cancer, AIDS, or the so-called war on drugs. In these cases, we can witness firsthand the failure of our rational logic.

You need to recognize how much you limit yourself when you rely only on that logic, and how that cuts you off from simpler, more effective solutions. The pure rationalist, of course, will object to the word "simple." To him, nothing important can be simple. To that person, I suggest revisiting the quote by physicist John Wheeler at the beginning of this book. And I'll add to this; his thinking is behind the times. What he may not have noticed is that today's most advanced Western science, especially theoretical physics, is finally recognizing the same paradoxical, analogical ways of thinking that have been part of Eastern traditions for thousands of years. And these don't contradict the core principles of Christianity either.

In the end, the choice is yours: Will you make yourself a powerless person? Or a powerful one? You decide. It's your life. Not mine.

Part Two:
The Unshakeable Foundations of
The LO^{2}LA Principle

1. How Humans Work

"And there is nothing in the world I know less about than myself, about Siddhartha!"
—Hermann Hesse, Siddhartha

The LO^{2}LA Principle is built on a very specific view of human nature, which I'll outline in this chapter. Daily life makes one thing clear: we'll only begin to solve our problems when we align ourselves with this view of what it means to be human. However, daily life also reveals something else: we rarely adhere to these principles. And as a result, our problems don't get smaller; they grow.

If you want to make real progress in your personal life, the key is simple: begin living in accordance with this human image. Don't just reflect on the principles, put them into practice every day

1.1 The Most Radical Principle

"I want to learn from myself, want to be my student, want to get to know myself, the secret of Siddhartha."
—Hermann Hesse, Siddhartha

In my presentations, I often ask a simple question: "Who or what needs to change if we want to improve a given situation?" Almost without fail, the spontaneous answer is: "The change has to start with me."

Strange, isn't it? Because in practice, we behave quite differently. Experience shows that we usually expect others to change.

Employees expect the boss to change. Bosses expect the employees to change. Citizens blame the government. Governments blame the citizens. Business owners want lower interest rates. Savers want higher ones. In 1993, the French wanted the Germans to lower their interest rates to boost the French economy. And Mrs. Smith is convinced that Mrs. Davis is raising her children all wrong and should really change.

Karl Marx believed that society needed to change for people to change. But isn't society made up of people? Even the United Nations seems to believe that it's always certain people, governments, or nations that need to change.

Generally, it goes like this: the "virtuous" expect others, the obviously less virtuous, to improve. And because everyone assumes that someone else must change, nothing changes. It's a stalemate, a standstill fueled by the endless shifting of responsibility and power onto others.

It's a curious contradiction: logically, we all agree that change begins with ourselves. But our actions say the opposite. We're always waiting for someone else to go first.

Many people believe they know exactly what others, politicians, businesses, and bankers, should be doing. Let's say someone is unemployed. If they blame their former employer, the government, the central bank, whoever, they drastically reduce their chances of finding a new job. Why? Because they've made themselves powerless. They've handed their fate to someone else. And if they sit around waiting for others to change, they could be waiting a long time.

And please don't call this theory. I was unemployed myself in the 1970s. I didn't blame my boss or the economy. I turned the spotlight on myself. I took full responsibility for my situation, and I found a new job quickly. Had I blamed everyone else, I might have stayed unemployed for a long time. This isn't history; I still observe the very same thing happening today.

Believing that others need to change only leads to more conflict and more problems. Relationships fall apart and situations worsen as a result.

Look at Soviet communism: at its core was the belief that others, entire populations, had to be reformed, even against their will. The result? Suppression, suffering, conflict, and war. The same attitude has kept the Gaza region in a death grip, even today.

What holds true on the level of nations also applies to individuals: if you think you can solve your problems without changing yourself, you're mistaken. Some people would literally rather die than change. Remember the man with the heart transplant?

Apparently, it's easier to blame others than to take a hard look at yourself. But when you start changing, something extraordinary happens: the outside world begins to change with you (more on this later). When you change, the world changes. That's real power!

This is the most radical core principle one can think of, and the one behind everything in this book: Change truly must begin with you.

It's ancient wisdom. We all know the saying: "If everyone swept in front of their own door, the whole world would be clean."

But where is the United Nations sweeping? Where are the virtuous? The ethical committees? The political parties? Are they sweeping in front of their own doors?

Nearly 1,000 years ago, this principle was captured impressively in a Confucian text:

"To put the world in order, we must first put the nation in order; to put the nation in order, we must first put the family in order; to put the family in order, we must first cultivate our personal life; we must first set our hearts right."

It really is that simple. And yet, somehow, it feels so difficult.

This is why our politicians can never truly solve our problems. By definition, a politician concerns themselves with other people's affairs. Just look at how many governments and institutions interfere in the business of other countries. But none of that needs to concern you. What others do is their problem. What matters is what you do. You can solve your problems and reach your goals by acting in alignment with your true power. Everything else is noise.

There is only one person in the world who truly needs to change, and that person is you.

Let's leave everyone else in peace.

1.2 Free Will

Man, every man, is bestowed with free will. You might say, "So what? What's the big deal?"

It's a very big deal.

Free will means that we can think whatever we want. We are not slaves to our thoughts; we are their masters. Just pause and consider that: you can think whatever you want. That is not something to take for granted. It's the source of your freedom. And with that freedom comes power. We'll explore this connection in more detail in a later chapter.

For now, I want to make one thing clear: free will isn't some abstract philosophical idea. It is, in my view, the greatest gift life has given us. It allows you to form your own thoughts about the world, about life, about others, and, most importantly, about yourself. And we all use this power, either for our benefit or to our own detriment.

For example, some people see the world as a "valley of tears." Others see it as full of exciting opportunities.

Some think Peter is a petty gossip. Others see him as a loving family man. Same world. Same Peter. Different thoughts. Why? Because we all have free will.

And that means everything is possible. War is possible. Peace is possible. Sickness is possible. So is health. Wealth is possible. So is poverty.

So, when people cry out during times of war or famine: "How could this happen? How could God allow it?", they're missing the point. It's not that God can allow it. It's that God must allow it, because of free will. That's the deal.

But this brings with it something else: total responsibility. The freedom to think whatever we want also means we are responsible for our thoughts. And our thoughts influence how we feel, and ultimately how we act. Freedom and power always come with responsibility.

If you choose to believe the world is a terrible place, no one forced you to. That's your choice, and you must live with the consequences. Even if eight billion others agree with you, you still have the power to think differently. That responsibility is yours, and so are the results. We'll explore this more deeply in the chapter on Action = Reaction.

Free will also means something surprising: no one, no higher being, no alien, no Messiah, has the right to save you against your will. If a person chooses destruction, they have that right. It's built into the system. But they also must live with the consequences of that choice.

Take this idea to its logical conclusion, and something else becomes clear: the future cannot be predicted. Doesn't this make perfect sense? Because of free will, any person can change their thoughts at any time. And when thoughts change, so do actions, and so does the future.

You might say, "But aren't there people who can predict the future?" Yes, but only because people tend to stay the same. Predictions only come true when no one changes their thinking. But the moment you do, the course of your life shifts. What a clairvoyant may have seen no longer applies.

When my wife was a child, a fortune teller told her she would never marry and never have children. She's been married for a while and has two sons. That prediction was wrong because she chose differently. The future isn't written in the stars or your palm or the tea leaves. It's written in your thoughts. Your free will shapes it.

This has enormous implications. It means that neither your life nor humanity's future is predetermined. It cannot be predetermined. That would violate the law of free will. Destiny is not something that happens to us. It's something we create. We happen to destiny! If you choose to give your power away to fate, horoscopes, or predictions, then yes, those things may govern your life. But only because you let them. You shape your life. Not fate. Not destiny. Not tradition.

The principle of free will changes everything. It is a universal law. And like all true laws, it arises from love, unconditional love, because only unconditional love gives others the right to think freely. Without control. Without interference. Free will and unconditional love are two sides of the same coin. One cannot exist without the other.

What you see in a person, you become; God, when you see God, Dust, when you see Dust.

The choice is always yours. You have the free will to become either.

1.3 Human Potential

In this chapter, we aim to answer two fundamental questions:

1. What does human potential consist of?
2. Is human potential limited or unlimited?

The answers are essential to everything that follows.

What is Human Potential?

Human potential, your potential, rests on two essential pillars: energy and intelligence.

Physicists have shown that everything is energy. You are energy. I am energy. A tree is energy. A table is energy. Nothing happens without energy. We can't move, create, or achieve anything without it. The less energy we have, the harder it becomes to reach our goals or solve problems. The more energy we have, the more effortlessly we do both.

Naturally, the LO²LA Principle must address these key questions:

Where does your energy come from?

Where are you losing or blocking energy?

How do you unlock and maximize your energy?

For companies, the goal is to maximize the collective energy of all employees and channel it toward clear, meaningful objectives. Leadership, then, becomes a question of energy management.

There is a kind of behavior that unleashes our highest energy, and with it, our greatest power. We'll explore that in detail.

But energy alone isn't enough. We also need intelligence that helps us make the right decisions. I'm not talking about school smarts or technical know-how. I mean a deeper intelligence that exists independently of education, and that is available to everyone. Whether we're talking about governments, businesses, or individuals, success depends on making more 'right' decisions than 'wrong' ones, and that, in turn, depends on our ability to access this universal intelligence.

So, the LO²LA Principle must also help answer:

How do I access this intelligence?

How do I get the right answers to my most important questions?

Is human potential limited?

To answer that, let's return to the two core elements: energy and intelligence.

Is energy limited? No. Energy is vibration, and vibrations can be shifted, expanded, and elevated.

Is intelligence limited? Where are its boundaries? Can you define them?

Energy and intelligence are inherently unlimited, which means human potential is also unlimited. The real question is: how do we activate and expand it?

The brilliance of the universal laws is this: there is a kind of behavior that leads to both maximum energy and maximum intelligence. That's what the LO²LA Principle is all about.

The Two Realities of Human Nature

Swiss physician and psychiatrist Balthasar Staehelin proposed a compelling view of human nature in his book, *Die Welt als Du (The World as You)*, one that also underlies my observations. According to Staehelin, every person operates within two realities:

1. The first reality: The limited self

This is the realm of rational thought, analysis, and planning, I call it "head thinking." It's where we attempt to grasp and control the future using logic alone. But since we can never know the future with certainty, this realm is filled with doubt, fear, and anxiety. Will it work out? Will it fail? The head doesn't know, of course, but it imagines misfortune, accidents, and catastrophes in the most creative ways.

As Staehelin notes, this is also the source of nearly all our personal and societal problems. Our heads try to judge, categorize, and explain everything, only to entangle us deeper in conflict.

Just look around: despite our staggering accumulation of knowledge, the world today has more problems than ever. If our intellect were truly capable of solving life's challenges, wouldn't we be living in a problem-free paradise by now? Contrary to our superstitions, our rational thinking is extremely limited.

The harsh truth is: we cannot solve the problems of infinite life with finite thinking. And we cannot access infinite potential with a finite tool. That's why things are not working out for us.

This first reality is often described as the "masculine" one: logic, control, competition, and domination over others. It is mainly materialists who cling to these values. The former Soviet Union presents a good example of where such masculine-centric materialism can lead. Let's not forget that the official philosophy of Russian communism was founded on the theory of materialism as elaborated by Marx and Engels. For Marx, there was nothing but ever-changing matter. The consequences of such limited thinking are extremely uncomfortable for those affected by it. Such failed ideologies are clear hints of what happens when we reduce ourselves to this head-centric worldview in our thinking.

2. The Second Reality: The Unlimited Self

Thankfully, this is not the whole story. Every human being also has access to a second reality, a realm beyond limits.

This is the realm of intuition, synthesis, wholeness, the inexplicable, and the eternal present. There is no analysis, no judgment, no separation. What this is about is unity and simplicity, not duality and complexity. No conflicts or problems arise from this place. And because there's no focus on the past or future, there's no fear, no guilt, no doubt, only trust. Trust in life, trust in universal intelligence, trust in something greater than ourselves. Whether you want to call it "God" or something else is entirely up to you.

I call this second realm "heart thinking." Here, the heart and our intuition speak. We have tried for an eternity to split the head from the heart. We've been taught to ignore it. We've forcefully elevated intellect and diminished intuition. We've glorified our tiny logic and fallen for the illusion that it would be enough to solve all our problems. Is it really surprising that heart attacks and strokes are on the rise when we disconnect our heart and overload our head?

Using this second intelligence, we could solve all our problems. As it is limitless, it has access to all the information there is—an impossibility for our mind. And yet, the majority of humanity continues to rely on the limited information available to the head for their decision-making.

The qualities that arise from this second reality are often described as feminine: heart, feeling, intuition, and unity. It is interesting in this context that women are increasingly taking on more active roles in various aspects of life. This trend will undoubtedly continue, and must continue. The traditionally "masculine" qualities have yielded impressive material results, but they have faltered when it comes to addressing our deeper problems. What we need now are more of the "feminine" qualities. It seems that, for a long time, the masculine was praised as strong and glorious, while the feminine was dismissed as weak, irrational, or even foolish.

A woman once told me that she often had to make decisions in meetings with men. Intuitively, she always felt she knew what was right. But the men would immediately ask her how she arrived at her opinion and whether she could prove or explain it, a classic example of first-reality thinking. She had to admit she couldn't explain "it," and so she often felt stupid. The men, after all, could explain everything, and she could not. But in truth, she had tapped into a far more comprehensive intelligence. The men, by contrast, were relying solely on the narrow, limited intelligence of the head.

Beyond Gender

To avoid any misunderstanding: these two realities, limited and unlimited, have nothing to do with the biological difference between man and woman. Both realities exist in every human being. It's just that some people are more practiced at accessing one over the other.

Let's summarize: Every person consists of both a limited and an unlimited intelligence. It is up to the individual, guided by the principle of free will, to decide which of these two intelligences to rely on. In this book, I am interested in one essential question: How do I activate this universal intelligence within me? Or put another way: How do I listen to the "God" within?

The LO²LA Principle offers a simple, clear answer to this question. If it didn't, you could throw this book away.

The consequences of the view of humanity briefly outlined here are immense. They influence all areas of life. I will return to this again and again throughout the book.

So, let us conclude our reflections on the nature of the human being with this:

Every person has unlimited potential, consisting of energy and intelligence.

Every person has free will. The only person you truly need to change is yourself.

2. How the Universe Works

Everything is vibration/energy. Matter is not the actual reality; vibration/energy is. This has been confirmed by physicists, especially in the field of nuclear physics. And this fact has far-reaching consequences for our lives.

If everything is energy, then our thoughts are also energy, which means they have the power to influence the external world. Thoughts aren't just something that happen inside our heads. Their effects go far beyond that. We'll explore the full implications of this in the chapter titled Action = Reaction.

If everything is energy, then human beings are energy as well. And that leads to two fundamental conclusions: First, human beings can develop themselves at will. Second, human beings are immortal. Energy cannot be destroyed.

Let's take a closer look. When you supply energy to a body, its frequency increases. That means the body changes state. Ice becomes water. And if you continue to add energy, water turns to steam. And even though you can no longer see it, nothing has disappeared; everything is still present.

That's physics. And what applies to ice and water also applies to people. If a person raises their vibration high enough, the moment will come when they are no longer visible to the human eye. This has nothing to do with mysticism or magic. It's just physics. If a person becomes "invisible," it simply means that they've transformed their dense physical body into a finer, subtler one. There is no death. The idea of death is a limited, materialistic notion we've imposed on ourselves, and now we live with the consequences.

Over two thousand years ago, Jesus tried to show us that death does not exist. "Death, where is your sting?" he asked. But few truly understood what he meant. One who did is nuclear physicist Jean-Émile Charon. One of his books is titled *J'ai Vécu quinze milliards d'années*, which translates to *I Have Lived 15 Billion Years*. That's the estimated age of the universe, and for him, death is not real either.

So, if a human being is "vibration", then this vibration can be changed, consciously and deliberately. How? The answer is simple: through our thoughts. We change our body's vibration with our thinking. This is easy to verify. Think loving thoughts. Now think hateful thoughts. The effect on your body is radically different because each thought vibrates at a different frequency. One makes us tense up, while the other makes us open up.

We can think ourselves deep into dense matter; many people do this every day, or we can think ourselves "into heaven." The choice is ours. That's the power of free will.

And because everything is vibration, illness is nothing more than a disturbance in vibration. Which means other vibrations can influence it. Music, color, scent, and of course, thought, can all alter our inner frequency.

This insight is nothing new. Novalis, the poet and mystic of the Romantic era, expressed it beautifully: "Every illness is a musical problem." In other words, a vibrational problem since music is sound and sound is vibration. It follows, then, that illness can be healed through thought. Jesus showed us this, too.

Everything is energy, and therefore, everything is vibration. That includes human beings. Imagine a person as a musical instrument. If it's out of tune, it produces discordant sounds, just like a person out of tune produces conflict, frustration, or aggression. Surely, you've heard someone say: "She's not in harmony," or "He's off balance." That's not just a figure of speech. Our task is to re-tune this human instrument, using our thoughts. No one else can do this for us. Each person is responsible for their own thinking, and therefore for the harmony or disharmony they emit into the world.

I'm always struck by how much wisdom is hidden in language. Take the word "person." It contains the Latin root per-sonare. Sonare means "to sound," so personare means "to sound through." A person, then, is something that "sounds through." Once again: vibration. In French, le son also means sound. Every person is a tone, one that can be changed, refined, or distorted.

If you want to solve your problems effectively and achieve your goals with greater ease, you must keep one thing in mind at all times: everything is vibration, and therefore, everything is changeable.

Even concrete is vibration, so it can change. That difficult employee is vibration and can change. That autistic child is vibration, and can change, no matter what conventional medicine may claim.

Of course, from the perspective of a purely materialistic medical system, many things are incurable and unchangeable. But that belief does not align with the countless examples of healing (including those demonstrated by Jesus), nor with what nuclear physics tells us. When we cling to materialist explanations, we not only waste time and money, but we also turn our backs on the deeper universal laws. We should stick to foundational truths. And one such truth is this: Everything is vibration.

There's further evidence in our language. Take the word "reality." It breaks down into Re and Al. In ancient Egypt, Re (or Ra) was the sun god, a symbol of energy and vibration. The sun gives light and warmth. Light is energy, and energy is vibration. And Al points to All, the universe, or in Islam, to Allah, the divine. So "reality" becomes divine light, divine vibration. That's what it is. That's all there is.

This is reality.

Keep this in mind as you move through life. It is up to you to think yourself down into the heavy darkness of matter, or up into the light. You, and no one else.

That is reality. Everything else is superstition, ignorance, or small-minded thinking.

If you believe the world is a valley of tears, then think yourself downward. So be it. If you believe the world is a festival of joy, then think yourself upward. So be it.

This is not mysticism. This is not religion. It is physics, pure and simple.

2.1 There Is No Objective World

"I have found a thought, Govinda, which you will again take as a joke or as folly, but it is my best thought. This is it: The opposite of every truth is just as true!"
—Hermann Hesse, Siddhartha

For decades, we've been taught that there is such a thing as an objective world, a world that can be measured precisely, and that is the same for everyone. In other words, there is only one world. This belief is so deeply ingrained that many people find it nearly impossible to think otherwise. It's another clear example of how rarely we question what we've been taught. We've been thoroughly conditioned to accept a specific worldview: that of an external, objective reality common to all.

But here's the truth: That world does not exist.
Using insights from both physics and neurobiology, I will now attempt to dismantle this outdated idea, because it

keeps us from solving our problems, and because it turns us into victims of a rigid, inherited worldview.

Over the past century, everything has increasingly pointed toward a different reality. The shift may have begun with quantum physics. Physicists discovered that "something" can appear either as a particle or a wave. And what it appears to be depends on the observer. This was a groundbreaking realization. It means that the observer influences what is observed. And that, in turn, means there is no single, objective world that is the same for everyone.

A bit more recently, French nuclear physicist Jean-Émile Charon, who extended Einstein's theory of relativity, put it this way: "Le monde n'est pas, il est ce qu'on pense de lui." Translated: "The world does not exist; it is what we think of it."

Imagine that. The world is what you think it is. This turns the old worldview on its head, and that has consequences.

Because if the world is what you think of it, then you are not a helpless bystander in some fixed reality. You are not at the mercy of a "good" or "bad" world. Quite the opposite: the world is at your mercy. You define your world. You shape it. That is power.

What do you think of the world? Whatever it is, that's what your world becomes.

There is not just one world. There are as many worlds as there are people. Each person lives in their own world, created by their thoughts. If we really understand this, we're led to a simple but surprising question:

Who would be foolish enough to imagine a bad world?

Apparently, many people. Obviously, all those who have never questioned the myth of the objective world. All those who have fallen for one of the most damaging errors in human history.

The realization that each person's world is shaped by their own thinking carries implications we haven't even begun to grasp fully. To help you get a sense of just how powerful this is, try replacing the word "world" with other expressions:

My wife is what I think of her.

My husband is what I think of him.

My children are what I think of them.

My employees are what I think of them.

My boss is what I think of her.

My customers are what I think of them.

The recession is what I think of it.

The pandemic is what I think of it.

Can you feel the enormous power contained in this insight? You can continue this exercise endlessly.

And if you're thinking, "That's just a theory," then congratulations, you've just proven the point. The book you're holding is also just what you think of it. If you think it's nonsense, then it's nonsense. If you think it's brilliant, then it's brilliant.

It's not the book that determines what it is. You do!

Don't misunderstand me, of course, there are objective measurements. One person is 5'11", another is 5'7". So yes, one is objectively taller than the other. But that's not what we're talking about here. We're talking about the effect, the emotional response something triggers. That's the true reality.

To one person, someone who's 5'11" may seem tall; to another, they may seem average. Everyone has their own truth. And that truth comes from within; it's a feeling.

So, when physics tells us that there is no objective world, it also tells us: there is no single truth. There are many truths. You can't argue about the truth, because there isn't just one. Everything you believe to be true is true for you. If someone else believes the opposite, that is their truth.

This single insight would bring an end to most conflicts and wars. Because if we understood that there is no one ultimate truth, we would stop trying to impose our version of it on others. This idea is not new; it's part of Eastern wisdom, which teaches that the opposite of a profound truth is another profound truth. Put simply: Nothing is true. Everything is true.

The only question that really matters is: Does your truth support or hinder your growth?

With the LO²LA Principle, I want to offer you a truth that will support your development, if you choose to accept it. And again, if you think that this is all just theory, you're right. And by thinking that, you make yourself weak, a victim of your own mind. And if that's what you choose, then so be it. That's your right. But from my point of view, it's not a very smart choice. Because what kind of person voluntarily gives up their power and becomes a helpless victim? To surrender your power like that, voluntarily, is a level of self-limitation that's hard to beat.

Here's the paradox: The human being, endowed with unlimited potential, voluntarily turns themselves into a powerless creature. Now that is an achievement!

And it's not just physics pointing us in this direction. Neurobiology provides similar evidence. Two researchers, Humberto Maturana and Francisco Varela, came to a similar conclusion in their book *The Tree of Knowledge*: "There is no external, objective truth. No universal truth." For Maturana and Varela, too, reality depends on the observer.

The 14th-century mystic Abd al-Karim al-Jili wrote: "People are like mirrors facing each other."

In other words, we always see ourselves in others. Our own thinking is reflected back at us. We can go a step further and say: the entire world is a mirror.

When you look at it, you see yourself: Aggression, if you are aggressive. Peace if you are peaceful.

You and I create the world through our thinking.

But what do we usually do instead? We try to find out who we are, or what our employees are capable of, by analyzing ourselves or others. And that too is based on the false assumption of an objective world. There is no such thing as an objective person.

You are what you think of yourself. Period.

Your employees are what you think of them. Period.

Your customers are what you think of them. Period. Decide for yourself what you want to think about yourself, your employees, your family, your world. But once you do, take full responsibility for those thoughts.

If you do that, you can forget all the analysis. It's more efficient. It saves time and money. The universe operates with breathtaking efficiency (which is especially fascinating for an economist like me). Only human beings have managed to complicate everything beyond reason. Fortunately, we've now made things so complex that we're reaching a breaking point. Sooner or later, we'll have to find a new way of seeing if we want to survive.

And if we don't survive? That's not a tragedy. Because as we now know: Death doesn't exist.

Now you know how the world works. You change the world with your thinking. That gives you unimaginable power. Use it as you will. You have free will, after all.

2.2 Everything Is One

"He could no longer distinguish the many voices, could not distinguish the gay from the weeping, the childish from the virile; they all belonged together, the yearning laments and the wise man's laughter, the cry of anger and the moans of the dying; they were all one, all of them interlinked and interwoven, bound together in a thousand ways."

—Hermann Hesse, Siddhartha

The previous chapter was probably already quite a stretch for some readers. But now it goes even deeper. Just like the idea that there is no objective world, the notion that "All is ONE" is something that's not taught in any official school system, at least not yet. But I'm confident that these concepts, already familiar to both physicists and mystics alike, will find their way into school curricula within the next hundred years. And what are a hundred years in the infinity of time?

The feeling of separation is one of the biggest challenges many people face. I'm talking here of feeling disconnected from other people, from nature, or even from life itself. But this feeling of separation is an illusion, a human construct. In reality, separation doesn't exist. This false sense of separation comes from "head thinking" (see Chapter 1.3). "Heart thinking", on the other hand, knows nothing of separation. So, the belief in separation is actually a sign of how disconnected the head and the heart have become. You can clearly see this disconnection in those suffering from addiction; they are hit the hardest.

But we now know, from both ancient mystics and modern scientists, that separation is an illusion. In truth, the universe is a unified whole. Everything is connected. Everything is entangled with everything else.

In theoretical physics, there's a well-established principle known as "Bell's Theorem." In 1964, physicist J.S. Bell demonstrated that "no theory of reality compatible with quantum theory can assume that spatially separated events are independent of each other." What does that mean? It means that nothing in the universe is truly separate from anything else, not people from each other, not humans from nature, not even events that are light-years apart.

Put simply, information about the whole is available at every single point in the universe. Every human being, then, holds within them all the knowledge in the universe and has access to omniscience. This isn't new; Eastern sages have been saying this for centuries. And now, the insights of nuclear physics are confirming it. French nuclear physicist J.E. Charon said it this way: "Every atom is connected to every other atom in the cosmos through the substance (spirit!) of antimatter... All knowledge is potentially accessible to every atom in the universe." What Einstein called "spooky action at a distance" highlights the non-local nature of quantum physics.

These scientific findings are staggering, but they haven't yet found their way into mainstream thinking, despite having massive implications on your life, my life, the life of a salesperson, etc.

It began back in the 1920s, when quantum physics flipped the natural sciences on their heads (remember: there is no objective world). If we took these discoveries seriously, it would revolutionize our lives. Chaos researcher and physicist Paul Davies once said, "Like the theory of relativity before it, [quantum theory] swept away many deeply rooted assumptions about the nature of reality." In other words, reality is not what we thought. There is no separation, only unity. That is the real nature of things.

And this isn't some obscure academic idea; it has real, everyday implications. The solution to most of our problems lies in this truth.

Just imagine: nothing that happens in the world, or even in the universe, is separate from you. And the reverse is also true: whatever you do has an effect on the entire universe. Do you feel the weight of that responsibility? What you do, and even what you think, impacts not just your family or your business, but the whole world.

Are you powerless? Or are you powerful? We keep coming back to the same core truth: human beings possess unimaginable power.

Mystics have long known that everything is ONE. Today, many physicists acknowledge that everything is ONE.

Zen Buddhism teaches the same thing. The symbol of this idea is the hand-drawn circle. It represents unity. It's not "either/or," it's "both/and."

In contrast, the symbol of our modern way of thinking isn't a circle; it's the straight line. A line drawn with a ruler, slicing things apart like a knife. It represents our linear, dualistic, "either/or" mindset. German filmmaker and author Herbert Achternbusch had a great image for this: "the highway in our brains." Imagine a straight line with arrows on both ends, pulling in opposite directions. That's conflict. That's duality. That's Aristotelian logic: "either/or."

But our problems will never be solved with that logic because reality doesn't work that way. Reality is unity, not separation. Separation leads to conflict, and conflict wastes time and energy. It is deeply inefficient and hence not economic.

You might say, "But I'm not a Buddhist, I don't follow Eastern philosophy." Fair enough. But maybe you're familiar with Christianity. And here's the surprising thing: Jesus knew that everything is ONE, too. Of course, living 2,000 years ago, he didn't have the language of quantum physics. So he used imagery and parables to convey complex truths. Jesus said: "Truly I tell you, whatever you did for one of the least of these brothers and sisters of mine, you did for me." And "I and the Father are ONE."

These statements only make sense if he knew the reality of unity. Otherwise, it's nonsense. So, the idea of oneness is not exclusive to Eastern traditions; it's at the heart of Christianity, too. And so is love. In fact, as we'll see, love cannot be understood apart from the idea of unity. The two go hand in hand. Jesus' teachings are remarkably coherent when seen in this light.

You may have also heard of this remarkable experiment: A measuring device was connected to a plant. Then, some distance away, live shrimp were dropped into boiling water. What happened? The plant reacted measurably. This is only possible if there is no real separation, if there is a communication, a connection, an entanglement.

This experiment brings Jesus' words into sharp, visceral focus.

There's also a martial art rooted in this concept of unity: Aikido. Because it's based on the principle of oneness, there are no winners or losers in traditional Aikido. That's why it's not part of the Olympics. But there's something powerful here: a trained Aikidoka, a master of Aikido, is nearly impossible to defeat. Why? Because they're operating from unity. From power. From harmony.

The LO²LA Principle shows you how to become an "Aikidoka" in your own life, invincible, not because you fight, but because you no longer divide.

Everything is ONE. And the consequences of this truth, for your life, are immeasurable.

2.3 Total Communication

Let's take a moment to consider a profound consequence of the fact that everything is ONE: total communication.

Books, seminars, and workshops overflow with advice on how to communicate better. There are countless trainings in marketing, advertising, presentation skills, sales strategies, public speaking, and more. But all these techniques only scratch the surface. They deal with what we might call conscious communication—just the tip of the iceberg.

What rarely gets discussed is the far larger, far more influential realm of unconscious communication.

If we take the two core principles seriously, "Everything is vibration" and "Everything is ONE", then the conclusion is simple but staggering: there is total communication in the universe. Everything is in constant communication with everything else, whether we like it or not. No one is isolated. No one can isolate themselves.

This has dramatic consequences for everyone, but especially for those in leadership, management, or sales. The LO²LA Principle is built on this insight. In fact, many of the problems people face today are impossible to solve without an understanding of total communication.

Just think about it: You are constantly communicating with everything in the universe, and the universe is constantly communicating with you. The only question is: "Are you listening?"

For many nuclear physicists, this isn't surprising at all. J.E. Charon put it bluntly: "Who, in our supposedly advanced civilization, is still capable of understanding the language of stones and trees?"

To a nuclear physicist, it's obvious: stones and trees speak. The entire universe 'speaks'. And since you and I are part of the universe, we too are part of this ongoing, universal conversation.

You might be wondering: "How does this help me pay my mortgage? How does this help me lose weight? How does this help me fix my marriage? How does this help me close more sales?"

It helps. More than you might think.

Because if everything is ONE, there is no true distance between you and your customers. No distance between you and your spouse. No distance between you and your banker, your boss, your child. Whatever you think, you are already communicating it to the people involved, instantly, wherever they are. Whether you're aware of it or not.

You influence the world with your thoughts. That's a fact. And if you want to solve your problems or reach your goals, then you must learn how to influence the world in a beneficial way.

We'll explore how to do that when we dive deeper into the LO^{2}LA Principle.

3. The Consequence: Our Problems Can Be Solved

I am firmly convinced that our problems can only be solved if we take the insights from this second part seriously and apply them consistently. If we do, not only can we solve our problems more efficiently, but we can also achieve our goals faster and with less effort than ever before.

Some people believe that certain problems or conflicts are unsolvable. And they're right, for two reasons: first, because the world is what they think of it. And second, because many problems cannot be solved with conventional thinking.

I, on the other hand, believe that all problems and conflicts are solvable. I'm also right, for two reasons: first, because the world is what I think of it. Second, because I propose a fundamentally different way of thinking.

Let me briefly summarize the principles I believe are essential:

Every person must begin with themselves. Stop trying to change others. Real change starts within.

Everyone has free will. We can choose our thoughts. And we can change them, any time. That means we can change our future.

Every person's potential is unlimited. If we want to overcome problems and reach our goals faster, we must begin tapping into this limitless potential.

Everything is vibration, everything is energy. That means everything can change. Nothing is fixed.

There is no objective world. The world is what we think it is. This gives each of us unimaginable power. We change the world with our thoughts.

Everything is ONE. The consequences of this realization are immense. When we understand this, conflict begins to disappear and with it, all the wasted time, energy, and resources that conflict creates. Solutions become easier. Goals become attainable.

We must move beyond "either/or" thinking. Life isn't black or white. The "both/and" mindset allows for deeper insight, creativity, and compassion. Judgment, by contrast, keeps us trapped. Let's be done with it.

But all of this depends on one thing: our willingness to break down the walls of our inherited belief systems. There is no other way forward.

Every human being has the power to rise above their circumstances. We were not born to toil for our bread endlessly, or to struggle against each other in survival mode. We were born to grow, to thrive, to experience joy and success.

Poverty, illness, and misfortune are not noble human qualities. Let's stop pretending they are.

The universe itself is abundance. The universe is health. The universe is joy. The LO²LA Principle, which I'll outline in the upcoming third part of this book, builds on everything we've explored in this second part. It also provides a way to overcome the limitations described in the first. When applied correctly, it leads to unimaginable power for you.

Part Three: The Mighty LO²LA Principle

"Knowledge can be shared, but wisdom cannot."
—Hermann Hesse, Siddhartha

The LO²LA Principle consists of three parts:

LO for Love, L for Letting Go, and A for Action = Reaction.

We begin with Action = Reaction, because this law forms the foundation for the entire principle. Without a clear understanding of what is meant by Action = Reaction, the concepts of Love and Letting Go remain incomplete. They cannot be fully grasped.

The 2 in the LO^2 is crucial. It represents the fact that a person's performance doesn't increase linearly with more love; it increases exponentially. Specifically, as a square.

You can read the word **LO²LA** like a formula:

Love^2 × Letting Go × A (where A = 1, because Action = Reaction is a neutral, constant law).

This formula expresses the performance a person can achieve.

Interestingly, it mirrors Ohm's Law, a foundational principle in electricity. According to Ohm's Law, when voltage (which we can equate to energy, or here, to love) increases, power increases by the square.

In other words: The same laws that govern the flow of electricity also govern the flow of life.

Just as electrical energy flows and transforms based on resistance, voltage, and current, the same is true for human energy and performance. Love is not just a feeling; it is a measurable force. When amplified, it leads to exponential results.

1. Action = Reaction

"Nothing is caused by demons. There are no demons. Everyone can perform magic, everyone can reach his goal, if he can think, wait, and fast."
—Hermann Hesse, Siddhartha

1.1 A Lesson in Physics with Consequences: How Our Thinking Works

In physics, we know the law of Action = Reaction. If I push against a wall with 10lbs of force, the wall pushes back with 10 lbs. If I push with 20lbs, it pushes back with 20 lbs. This chapter is about applying that same law, not to physical objects, but to our thoughts.

We're talking about thinking and its consequences.

What is a thought?

Since everything is vibration or energy, a thought is energy too. It's not "nothing," and it's not confined to the inside of your body. Human beings are perfect transmitters; they constantly send out thoughts. Each thought corresponds to a specific vibration—a specific energy potential—that radiates outward. A thought is a body of energy. It's important to visualize this. The stronger the energy of a thought, the greater its effect. There are strong thoughts, and there are weak ones. And because everything else is also vibration, thoughts can influence everything else.

Since every thought has energy, every thought has a tendency to materialize. The greater the energy behind it, the stronger that tendency.

The more powerful your thinking, the more likely it is to become real. Joy and enthusiasm, for example, are highly energetic thoughts that often lead to positive results. So positive thinking isn't magic; it has a physical basis. These energies naturally bring success with mathematical certainty. But remember: fear-based thoughts can be just as energetic. And those also tend to materialize, just as surely. That's why fear is never useful.

Let's take it one step further.

Similar thoughts carry similar vibrations and are attracted to each other. This leads to what we call "thought clusters" or "bodies of thought," which carry a far greater energy potential than a single thought. This has huge implications, not just for individuals, but for companies, nations, and humanity as a whole.

Let's say a company has 1,000 employees. All day, every day, these employees are thinking. Every single one of their thoughts matters. They combine to create an enormous pool of energy. If the general tone of those thoughts is positive, the company will thrive. If negative, results will reflect that. Management can try anything, but if most employees think negatively, the organization doesn't stand a chance.

A business can literally think itself into success or failure. And not just through its leaders, but through all its people. This is pure physics. Energy moves toward manifestation. In the end, management is really just energy management.

For me, the fall of the Berlin Wall is a powerful example of what happens when thought energy reaches a tipping point. That event was no coincidence. The wall came down when the collective thought energy of freedom finally outweighed the energy of oppression. Everything is a question of energy.

So, ask yourself honestly, "What kind of energy are you generating from morning to night?" You have free will. You can think whatever you want. But what you think determines the energy you release. What kind of energy do you want in your life?

Fear-based energy or love-based energy? This choice has deep implications.

Let's go another step deeper.

In physics, we know that energy cannot be lost. That's also true in the spiritual or mental realm. No energy is ever lost, meaning no thought is ever lost. Whatever you've thought, whatever you're thinking now, and whatever you will think, all of it remains. Every thought produces energy. And that energy always carries the potential to be realized.

Here's the crucial part: You can't undo your past thoughts, but thanks to free will, you can change your thoughts *now*. With new thinking, you send out new vibrations, new energies, and shape a new future. And now we arrive at the heart of this chapter:

Action = Reaction.

Every thought you send out comes back to you.

Sending a thought is an action. The reaction is what returns. Whatever you think, good or bad, returns to you. This is, in my view, the fairest and most just law in the universe. It's impartial and exact: You receive what you send out.

Let's look at some consequences.

Suppose you criticize someone. This law doesn't mean that the same person will criticize you. It means the quality of that criticism comes back to you, from somewhere. It might be someone else. Or a health issue. Or, in my case, a job loss.

Here's what happened to me: After college, I worked as an assistant to the CEO of a mid-sized company. Naturally, I thought I knew more than he. I had a degree; he didn't. I judged and criticized constantly. Eventually, things blew up. One day, I was out of a job. But I didn't blame my boss. I didn't blame the economy. I looked inward. I took responsibility. And I saw the energy I had released into the world. It came back to me, fully and forcefully. That, to me, is justice.

Now flip the situation: What if someone else criticizes or betrays you? Then they are the ones who will experience the consequences, not you. That's the genius of this law. You don't need to take revenge. You don't even need to think about revenge. The universe handles it.

That's why Jesus said, "If someone strikes you on the right cheek, turn to them the other also." Why? Because if you strike back, it will come back to you.

This law means you can't do anything better for yourself than to wish well for others. Whatever you do for others comes back to you. Paradoxically, the most "selfish" person is the one who wishes others the best. And the person who only looks out for themselves causes the most harm to themselves.

Isn't that incredible? I'm always in awe of the fairness of this universal law.

Imagine if more people lived by this law. Conflict would dissolve. You'd wish the best for others, knowing it circles back to you. And whether others follow it or not wouldn't matter because it's about your life, not theirs.

So, what do you want? Health? Happiness? Success? Prosperity? Then wish it for others, even strangers. Even people far away. Distance doesn't matter in the world of thought. Physics has confirmed this. Whether someone is in front of you or on vacation in Hawaii, your thoughts reach them. Think about the implications for families, companies, and even global conflict! Think about the implications for sales. A salesperson's thoughts about their clients matter, even from a distance.

This is not about belief. It's not faith. It's physics. Think of your thoughts like stones dropped into a lake. Ripples spread in every direction. And they always return to the source. As we are talking about the spiritual and not the material realm, there is no resistance, which means they return with the same energy they were sent out with. Therefore, take care of your thoughts.

In practice, an interesting pattern shows up. If you criticize someone who also criticizes you, the reaction takes longer. But if you criticize someone who hasn't wronged you, the reaction can be fast and brutal. I've seen people criticize a fired colleague, only to be fired themselves within months.

The more someone is embedded in materialism, the longer it can take for the reaction to arrive. That's why so many people believe in coincidence. But "coincidence" just means we can't see the connection, yet. If we had a wider perspective, like from an airplane, we'd see the links clearly. We'd see the reaction as the natural outcome of past thoughts, forgotten, perhaps, but never lost.

Sometimes the reaction is immediate. My wife once went into town with a friend. On the train, her friend complained incessantly about people's looks, clothes, and voices. When they got off the train, a drunk man walked by and spat on her sleeve. She was furious. She cursed the world. But what really happened? She had been "spitting" on others all morning, mentally. And now she received that same energy physically. Not by chance. Nobody is spat on by accident. Nobody is robbed or killed by accident. There is no coincidence in the universe.

There is a just law. The law of Action = Reaction. It is infallible. It has nothing to do with morality. It is neither good nor bad. It simply is. It is amoral. It always has been and always will be.

You create your reality through your thoughts. Everything you experience, everything, is authored by you. That means you can change everything. The visible world is the result of the invisible: your thoughts and your feelings.

Did you know this is the true meaning of the "Last Judgment"? "Last" just means "most recent." The judgment is now. It's what you face as a result of your past thoughts. Who else has the right to judge you, but you?

Your future depends on what you think now. So, in your own interest, and for the good of everyone, think only the best for yourself and for others.

You see, the universe is organized in an unimaginably simple way. So simple, in fact, that we often overlook it. And yet, this truth has been embedded in our language for ages. You've heard the saying, "What goes around, comes around." But let's not take that just materially. It also means: *As your thoughts go into the world, so your thoughts come back from the world.* Another one says, "You reap what you sow." The seeds are your thoughts, which you plant all day long. The harvest is what returns to you. It's that simple.

If your "harvest" is poor or unsatisfying, it's worth asking: What kind of "thought seeds" have I been planting? And if that gives you a chill, if you realize you haven't always thought noble thoughts, don't worry. Yes, your thoughts will return to you. But you can protect yourself from their full impact. The moment you begin to think positively and constructively, you shift your vibration. And that softens the reaction of any returning thought. If you could instantly switch to thinking in love, even the worst recoil would no longer harm you. Love is the highest vibration. It overpowers all others.

Jesus understood this law deeply. He didn't call it Action = Reaction; of course, that language wouldn't have made sense to people then. Instead, he said, "Judge not, lest ye be judged." What else is that but this universal law? If you judge (Action), you will be judged (Reaction). And it works in reverse, too: when you do good, good returns to you.

How does this apply to money? Interestingly, the German word for "spending" is Ausgabe, which contains Gabe, meaning "gift." So spending is actually a gift you give to someone else. If giving is the action, income is the reaction. Please carve this into your brain: Your income follows your outflow. Without giving, there is no receiving. What matters here is your attitude toward spending. If you spend reluctantly, you'll receive reluctantly. If you spend generously, you'll receive generously.

Hans C. Leu, one of the most successful hoteliers in Switzerland, put it well: "Those who count every butter roll get nowhere. Generosity should be a virtue for every host."

Action = Reaction. If your spending is stingy, don't be surprised when your income reflects that.

Let's take it a step further. When you buy something thinking, "That's too expensive," you're devaluing what you're about to receive. So, you receive less than what you paid for. That's how poverty is created. It's a direct result of your thinking. You create recession and personal financial decline through your internal valuation. Why? Because if you don't recognize the value of others' work (Action), your own work won't be recognized either (Reaction).

But the same law also creates wealth. When you say, "This is worth it," or "Great value," you affirm someone else's contribution. And your own contributions are affirmed in return. If you think, "I got more than I paid for," that's what you'll experience in life, over and over. The actual price doesn't matter. What matters is your perception of value. Poverty and wealth are not numbers; they're states of mind.

A painting company owner in France grew his business from 3 to 200 employees in 10 years. He explained his secret: "You have to give first if you want to receive." He paid above minimum wage. He gave gifts. He invested in people. They invested in him.

The worst thing a company or individual can do is to see everything as "too expensive" and tighten their purse strings. That's just another way of applying this law in reverse and triggering scarcity.

Please don't dismiss this as just nice ethics. It's not about morality. The universe doesn't deal in morality. Nature is not moral; it simply operates by law. Morality is a human invention, often used to control others. No one has the right to judge another human being. That contradicts the deepest teachings of Christianity.

This law is dangerous for those who don't know it. I lost a job because of it. One man I know lost half his eyesight in a few weeks because he didn't want to "see" his son-in-law anymore. As political groups rage against those who think differently, more conflict comes their way. But for those who do understand this law, it opens up extraordinary possibilities.

And remember, this law applies not only to individuals. It also applies to families, companies, nations, and all of humanity. The collective thinking of a group shapes its collective destiny.

What about disasters? There are two types:

1. Those that arise from natural universal events.

2. Those caused by human thought energy.

Much of the world's suffering is caused by the energy we produce. The Earth is sick from our thinking. If we're in inner conflict, of course, we see outer conflict. But we don't need to panic. Panic adds more energy to the problem. We just need to change our thinking.

Plastic in the ocean is not the real issue. Our thinking is the issue. The actual pollution is spiritual—our thoughts. Material pollution is only a reflection. As such, guard your thoughts. **Whatever we focus on grows.**

Here's another overlooked consequence of thinking: If thoughts are energy, then we are giving energy to whatever we concentrate on. This has enormous consequences.

If we focus on our weaknesses, they grow.

If we focus on illness, it grows.

If we focus on the lack of money, the lack increases.

If we focus on competition, it intensifies.

If we focus on violence or drug abuse, these problems multiply.

But the reverse is also true:

If we focus on prosperity, it grows.

If we focus on health, it improves.

If we focus on peace, peace expands. (In times of war, does anyone really focus on peace?)

What are you focusing on? What are you feeding with your energy?

Years ago, a man was attacked at a train station near my home. The story made the front page of the regional paper. Thousands of people read it, discussed it, and thought about the aggression in our world, adding even more energy to that aggression.

What most people missed is that thousands of people pass through that train station every day without incident. But we don't talk about that. We don't give that fact energy. One violent event gets all the attention, and so it grows.

Back in the '90s, Swiss television lamented that the number of drug addicts was rising, even after spending millions on anti-drug campaigns. However, the problem worsened. That campaign fed the issue fresh energy. You can't put out a fire by pumping in more oxygen. But that's what we do, privately and publicly.

The same principle applies in sports. An athlete who focuses on weaknesses rarely performs well. Champions are those who appreciate and utilize their strengths. Ignoring your weaknesses doesn't mean denial; it means not feeding them energy. That's how they shrink.

Yet many of us do the opposite. We willingly allow ourselves to be analyzed, assessed, and dissected to find our weaknesses. We think recognizing them helps us overcome them. But doing so either fails completely or requires massive effort. It's inefficient and uneconomical, and not how energy works.

Spiritual laws are fixed, incorruptible, and everywhere. Therefore, the only wise response is this:

No matter how your life looks right now, focus only on the upside. That's how you grow it. You don't need to fight darkness. Just turn on the light.

1.2 What is the World?
The Key to Human Power

We can be relatively brief here because we've already touched on this topic in Part Two, under the title "There is no objective world."

So, what is the world? The world is what you think it is.

That one sentence gives you unimaginable power. Once again, we're dealing with the law of Action = Reaction.

What does this mean for your life? It means: "What you believe to be true becomes true, for you."

Let's take two salespeople as an example. One says, "Our prices are too high." The other says: "Our prices are just right." Who's correct?

Both are. There's no such thing as an objective truth. Each person has their own truth. And recognizing this is the only solid foundation for constructive conversations.

If you walk into a meeting thinking in terms of "right" and "wrong," the result will be arguments, not progress.

You'll think you're right and the other person is wrong, and the other person will feel exactly the same. But if you approach the conversation with the understanding that everyone has their own truth, then you can actually get somewhere. You can ask: "Why does this salesperson believe the prices are too high?" And you can show them what that belief is doing to them. They're right, for them, the prices are too high. And their sales results will match that belief. That's almost certainly not the outcome they want.

Many years ago, I worked at a company with about 30 salespeople. One man in Munich consistently sold twice as much as everyone else. Why? The reason was simple: Before each year started, management set a target: around one million Swiss francs per salesperson. But the only thing that truly determined results was what each salesperson thought about that number.

Most of them thought, "It'll be tough, but I'll try."

The top performer thought, "A million? That's the minimum. I'm going for two." And that's what he achieved, year after year.

The others were right: it was hard. They barely hit their targets. The top seller was right, too: More was possible.

I can't change this truth:

The world is what you think it is.

The market is what you think it is.

Your customers are what you think of them.

You are what you think of yourself.

That's not wishful thinking, that's power. Real power. Let me show you how impactful this power can be:

First, people succumb to the fear of burglary (Action). Second, they get a guard dog (External sign of fear). Third, their home gets broken into (Reaction). Fourth, they feel validated in their initial fear, and so the cycle is perpetuated. Never mind that they simply fulfilled their own prophecy.

And here's the fascinating part: you always get confirmation of your beliefs. I call this the wheel of justice. Everyone is always right because they always end up proving themselves right.

There is more evidence that Jesus knew of this principle. He said, "According to your faith, be it done to you" (Matthew 9:29).

If you believe the world is dangerous, full of thieves and violence, so be it. If you believe the world is safe and peaceful, so be it. This is just another way of saying: Action = Reaction.

Try this: change your thinking about a certain person, a situation, or the world, and observe what happens. But give it time. If you've thought of your neighbor as a jerk for ten years, don't expect a miracle in one day.

Change your thinking and keep it changed. No matter what. You'll experience "miracles," or more accurately, universal laws at work. Why does this happen? Because: The world is what you think of it. And everything is ONE.

There's no real separation between you and your neighbor. You are your neighbor. Your neighbor is you. So, when you change, your neighbor must change. That's how oneness works.

And if you think this isn't true—that your neighbor will never change—then I have to agree with you. And so will the results: your neighbor won't change. Case closed.

You really are more powerful than you think, aren't you?

The astonishing thing about the law of Action = Reaction is that you apply it every single day, every hour, every minute, every second. Whether you want to or not, just like gravity, it's always at work.

Now that you know this, what advice would you give your child preparing for an exam?

Here's my recommendation: Encourage them to think, "I know," rather than "I don't know." It takes no extra effort but brings far greater rewards. That simple shift opens the door to the vast, universal intelligence inside each of us.

The thought "I don't know" closes that door.

If the world is what I think it is, then it makes far more sense to think, "I know," so that knowledge can come back to me.

1.3 Total Responsibility: Goodbye Coincidence

If you reflect on everything we've discussed, one conclusion becomes inevitable: You are responsible for everything that happens to you.

Please pay close attention to the second part of that sentence. You are not just responsible for what you do; that's nothing special. You are responsible for everything that happens to you because you are responsible for everything you think. And your thoughts determine your life.

So never again give your power away by saying, "He's responsible. I'm just the victim."

There are no victims in the universe. And there is no such thing as coincidence.

Many scientists have reached this same conclusion. Consider this: to randomly produce the enzyme Cytochrome c, a chain molecule made up of 104 amino acids, it would be like throwing 10^{130} dice and getting them all in the correct order. That simply could not have happened by chance.

By comparison, only about 10^{17} seconds have passed since the Big Bang. Even if one die had been rolled every second since the beginning of time, there still wouldn't have been enough time to create just that one enzyme randomly.

Yet so much of science continues to cling to the "god of chance," something that German music producer and journalist Joachim-Ernst Berendt describes in his remarkable book, *The World is Sound: Nada Brahma,* as "a psychological cramp."

Einstein put it more simply: "God does not play dice with the universe."

Physicist Paul Davies raises an equally important point when considering the principle of chaos: "How can you know whether tossing a coin or throwing dice is really random? There is no consensus on this." We should treat the concepts of coincidence and chance with more skepticism.

And no one plays dice with your life, except for one person: you. Everything that happens in your life has a cause. Coincidence would contradict every known law of life. And frankly, if we believed that randomness rules the universe, we'd be placing very little trust in its Creator. That would make for a bleak, senseless world.

The truth is, our thinking is too limited to perceive the full picture. We don't see all the causes, so we label events as "coincidence." Over a century ago, mathematician and physicist Henri Poincaré said: "A very small cause, which remains unnoticeable to us, produces a considerable effect that we absolutely must notice, and then we say that this effect depended on chance."

That effect might be a car accident. We say someone "accidentally" hit us. But we ignore the small, invisible cause, a thought we may have had long ago and since forgotten. From our limited, ground-level perspective, we see no pattern. But if we could zoom out, gain a bird's-eye view, we'd see how everything connects.

This brings us to a question many people ask in my seminars: Does this mean my birth wasn't an accident? That I didn't just happen to get the parents I got?

Exactly.

We're not talking about some man-made belief system here; we're talking about universal laws. Either coincidence exists or it doesn't. We don't get to pick and choose. And once we understand how ingeniously and elegantly the universe is structured, it becomes clear: there is no randomness, and certainly no injustice.

Think about how unjust it would be if people were simply born into their lives at random—some into privilege, others into suffering. If that were true, the universe would be governed by chaos, not intelligence. And it's no wonder that some people, unable to make sense of such a reality, fall into despair or even take their own lives.

But this is not how life works. Chance is an illusion. Birth is not random. To make sense of this, we must consider reincarnation—a concept embraced by millions across the world and originally part of early Christian teachings. In Buddhism, it's known as the Wheel of Life (Bhavacakra), and the goal is to break free from the cycle of rebirth by reaching enlightenment.

If we accept the commonly held view that a human being is made up of body, soul, and spirit, then, by analogy, the world must be similarly structured: a material realm (what we see), an astral realm (linked to the soul), and a spiritual realm (beyond the senses). Life moves between these realms. What we call "death" is merely birth into the astral world. What we call "birth" is death from that perspective.

We lay down our material body at a certain point and later take up a new one. Death, therefore, does not exist. Life cannot be killed or ended. It simply changes form. As Jesus said, "Death, where is your sting?" There is only life.

Every soul comes into this world with a purpose. To fulfill that purpose, certain conditions must be met, and we create those conditions by choosing our parents. In doing so, we also choose our race, our skin color, our location, and our nation. And we do this not by chance, but by free will.

This has profound implications.

Children are not "undeveloped" beings. In fact, they may be more spiritually evolved than their parents. And often, it's not the parents who are there for the children, but the children who are there to teach the parents.

I once heard a story of a woman who gave birth to a child with fetal alcohol syndrome. She had unknowingly consumed alcohol daily during the first two months of her pregnancy. When she learned she was pregnant, she stopped drinking, but by then, the damage was done. She was devastated.

How do we explain this without invoking coincidence or injustice? Do we believe the child is simply a random victim? Not if we accept reincarnation. The child chose that mother, perhaps to help her. And it worked: the mother stopped drinking. The child, who is not really a child in the spiritual sense, chose to take on this particular body to serve a greater purpose. That is boundless love. That is free will in action. And that is possible only because the soul knows life is eternal, and this physical existence is but a moment in the grand scheme.

According to some beliefs, a soul can wait up to 12 weeks after birth before it fully enters a newborn's body. In some cases, it may decide not to enter at all, which is what can happen in cases of sudden infant death syndrome. Medically, no cause is found, but the spiritual cause is simply that the soul chose not to live this life after all.

Keep in mind: the law of Action = Reaction applies across lifetimes. A reaction to something you did or thought might come not in this life, but in the next. Death is no boundary to this law; it's simply a transition.

Knowing this, no one should blame their parents for a difficult childhood. No one should justify harm done to others by saying, "Well, I had a rough upbringing." That kind of thinking gives away your power and violates the universal laws.

Each of us bears full responsibility for what we think, what we do, and what happens to us.

This is your power. And it's within your power to give it away, to your parents, to chance, or to some mysterious fate.

Jiddu Krishnamurti, one of the great thinkers of the 20th century, wrote: "If you are not prepared to feel responsible for everything, truly everything, that happens in your life, then you will not make any progress."

I have nothing to add, except to remind you that this is your choice. You have free will. You can keep spinning on the Wheel of Life, or progress towards stepping off. The decision is yours.

This concludes the foundational discussion of the LO²LA Principle as seen through the lens of the law of Action = Reaction.

2. Letting Go

"You don't force him, beat him, and give him orders because you know that 'soft' is stronger than 'hard,' that water is stronger than the rocks, that love is stronger than compulsion."

—Hermann Hesse, Siddhartha

My aim in this chapter is to show you how *letting go* can help you achieve your goals faster and with less effort than in any other way. In this context, however, I urge you to look at this topic not from a psychological perspective, but from a physical one; life is not a psychological "problem," life is a physical "problem" as we shall see. From a purely physical perspective, dimensions open up to us that we would never have thought possible.

2.1 The Power Over Life and Death

A 48-year-old plant manager "suddenly" fell ill. Six months later, the burly man was dead. The medical reason: cancer. The deeper reason: he couldn't let go.

A successful salesman worked for a service company. He was so good that he was able to retire at just 37. The apparent reason: he sold more than most. The deeper reason: he was exceptionally good at letting go.

At a luxury hotel in Switzerland, a man who didn't speak a word of German started working as a porter. Ten years later, he was the hotel's director. The apparent reason: he gave his best every day. The deeper reason: he knew how to let go.

I could give you countless examples. But the point is this: **Letting go** is about life and death, about happiness, prosperity, and success.

Life means movement. The ancient Greeks already understood this. Panta rhei, everything flows. And if life is truly "flow," then it's obvious: holding on leads to stagnation. And stagnation leads to death. What you hold on to stops moving. And whatever stops moving dies. Think of life as a river. A river that no longer flows becomes a pond. And stagnant water soon becomes stale and lifeless.

You want to know the quickest way to "kill" a marriage? Just hold on to your partner tightly enough. Don't let them move, don't let them breathe. Sooner or later, the marriage will suffocate. Please don't get me wrong, this is not an invitation to divorce!

Holding on for too long can also destroy a business. Take Kodak, for example. Once a giant of innovation and the undisputed leader in photography, Kodak filed for Chapter 11 bankruptcy in 2012. What happened? The company clung too tightly to its technology and its once-successful products. It held on for too long and locked itself out of the very market it helped create.

You can kill anything by holding on. It's only a matter of time.

Take archery, for instance. What do you need to do to hit the target? You need to draw the bow; that's energy. You need to aim; that's intelligence. And then you need to let go.

Anyone understands this when it comes to archery. But somehow, this basic principle doesn't seem so obvious when it comes to goals in everyday life. Try telling a traditional, hard-nosed manager that they'll reach their goals faster if they learn to let go. They'll probably look at you like you've lost your mind.

And yet, this is the truth:

Letting go is the fastest, most effortless, and most efficient way to reach any goal. And when I say, "any goal," I mean exactly that—any goal. Because we're not talking about a mindset or a strategy, we're talking about a universal law.

Now think back to the archer. What happens if she draws the bow but never lets go? At first, nothing. Then her arms begin to shake. She gets tired. Eventually, if she keeps pulling harder, the bow breaks.

And what do we say when someone gets sick from overwork or too much pressure? "She pushed herself too far." "She was stretched too thin."

If you overstretch the bow, you hurt yourself. You've held on too long. You've resisted the natural flow. And the result works against you. That's not just unhealthy, it's deeply uneconomical.

Letting go is life. Holding on is blockage, illness, and death.

Just as in the chapter on Action = Reaction, we're once again talking about power: your power over your own life and over what feels like death.

Now let's look more closely at what letting go really means, and how it works in detail.

2.2 Activating Our Universal Intelligence

We've established that human potential consists of two key forces: energy and intelligence. And we've also seen that if you want to reach your goals as quickly and effortlessly as possible, you need to use both at their maximum. The same applies to solving problems. If you want to solve a problem efficiently, you need to use your full intelligence and energy. It's simple logic, isn't it?

The purpose of this section is to explore how to activate your universal intelligence. Earlier, in section 1.3, we stated that every human being, without exception, possesses unimaginable intelligence.

So how do you access it? The answer is: by letting go.

Let's now take a closer look at what Letting Go actually means in practical terms.

If you have a problem or are aiming for a specific goal (**TARGET**), and I tell you to *let go,* what do I really mean?

1. Accepting the CURRENT state.

If you want to move from your **CURRENT** state to a **TARGET** state as quickly as possible, then logically, you cannot cling to the **CURRENT** state.

How can the **CURRENT** state transform if you're holding on to it? Holding on means blocking the change. Accepting it means releasing it, and then something remarkable happens: the **CURRENT** state starts to shift.

I often hear people say, "But I can't accept everything." I used to believe that too, and it almost destroyed me. But the truth is, you don't have a choice. You have to accept it. That's basic logic. What IS, *IS.* And once something IS, getting upset doesn't change it. What IS is simply the *NOW.* And no one can change what already is. We can influence the future, yes, but not the present moment.

When we refuse to accept what is, we create internal conflict. That conflict wastes energy, drains resources, and blocks our intelligence.

In other words: if you don't accept what IS, you're standing in your own way. And how can you solve problems or reach your goals if you're sabotaging yourself?

You might object: "But everyone fights the **CURRENT** state, even the Pope and the UN!" That's true. And that's exactly why most problems don't get solved. Instead, new ones are created.

You don't solve problems by fighting what IS. That's not psychology or philosophy, it's just physics and logic. Conflict creates resistance. Resistance wastes energy. And if the whole world operates through conflict and resistance, it's no wonder things don't improve.

Think of it like this: What would happen to your car if its shock absorbers didn't absorb the bumps in the road?

So first, no matter how bad things may seem, accept what IS.

2. Do not judge.

This ties directly into the first point. If you don't accept something, it means you're judging it. But the less you judge, the more easily you can accept. Letting go means not constantly labeling people and situations as good or bad. This principle aligns directly with the law of Action = Reaction.

Judging and condemning others creates blockages. And blockages lead to conflict. Conflict leads to resistance. This is physics. When you judge, you divide something that was whole, and division creates conflict and tension. And in a state of tension, you can't expect to achieve your goals quickly or easily. That's an illusion.

Yes, people still try to reach their goals through conflict. Maybe they have too much time or money. But that doesn't make it effective.

3. No fixation on the path.

Letting go activates universal intelligence. If you fixate on one particular path to a goal, you're limiting yourself.

That's pure head-thinking, and it blocks the heart, which is the seat of universal intelligence.

Your head might see one, two, maybe three paths to your goal. But who's to say there aren't hundreds more?

Many companies curb their employees' potential by imposing strict strategies to reach a target. Those strategies might work to a point, but they can't compete with a company that knows how to activate real intelligence.

Some of you may have heard of Professor Henry Mintzberg's study of the launch of Honda motorcycles in the U.S. The campaign was wildly successful largely because there was no fixed strategy. Traditional managers might panic at the thought, but those same managers rarely achieve anything truly extraordinary.

Honda's success came from having a clear goal but not tying its employees to one path to achieve it. Everyone was free to express their own intelligence.

To be clear: I'm not saying we should throw out all strategies. Strategies should act like guardrails, giving direction, not confinement, so people can unlock their full potential.

This principle also applies to health. When you're sick, your goal is (usually, but not always!) to recover. But if you fixate on a single therapy, you block your universal intelligence. Your heart, your life, your God knows better than your head how to heal. Why limit that?

Remember: you have free will. That means you can choose to deny this intelligence, even deny God. No one can heal you without your consent.

Let me give you a striking real-life example. In one of his well-known talks, Sir Ken Robinson shares the story of Gillian Lynne. You may not recognize the name right away, but you'll definitely recognize her work.

When Gillian Lynne was a young girl in the 1930s, her teachers were worried about her. She was fidgety, distracted, couldn't concentrate, and was disrupting the class. Today, she'd likely be diagnosed with **ADHD**. But back then, her mother was simply told that Gillian had a learning problem and needed to see a specialist.

So, her mother took her to a doctor. They talked about Gillian's issues for a while. Then, the doctor asked if he could speak to her mother privately. As they left the room, he turned on the radio. From outside, they watched Gillian: as soon as the music played, she was up and moving. The doctor turned to the mother and said something like, "She's not sick. She's a dancer. Take her to a dance school."

Thankfully, her mother did just that. Gillian walked into a room full of people like her—people who expressed themselves through motion. She later said it was the moment she felt she belonged. Gillian went on to train at the Royal Ballet, had a brilliant career as a dancer, and became one of the most successful choreographers in history, behind massive hits like Cats and Phantom of the Opera.

Sir Ken's point is sharp: someone else might've drugged Gillian, told her to calm down, to conform. But this doctor saw her differently.

History proves again and again how limiting fixed thinking can be. Treatments that were once considered criminal or insane are now standard practice. It will be the same 50 or 100 years from now.

Our "head thinking" is simply too limited to grasp all possible paths to success. If you want to rely solely on it, you're free to do so, just be prepared for the consequences.

4. No fighting against the CURRENT State or for the TARGET State.

Fighting means holding on. It means resistance. And resistance is a waste of energy and a block to intelligence. Yes, you can reach a goal through struggle, but at what cost? And with how much effort? If you're willing to pay that price, go ahead. Just be clear-eyed about the outcomes.

Look at the endless conflict between Israel and Palestine. What's the result? Massive effort, endless death, and immeasurable pain. That's not logic. That's not reason. It's ego, and ego is head-thinking.

By letting go, you can reach your goals faster and with less energy, even when the other side is stronger.

History gives us powerful examples. One of the most striking is Napoleon's failed invasion of Russia. Napoleon, a brilliant strategist with the most advanced army of his time, was unstoppable until he met his match in the Russian commander Kutuzov.

Against his officers' advice, Kutuzov didn't fight back. He let Napoleon march deeper into Russia, consuming his energy and morale. Kutuzov conserved his forces and refused to engage. Napoleon reached Moscow, assumed he had won, and sent peace offers. They were ignored. Then winter came. Kutuzov advanced and crushed Napoleon's exhausted forces. Napoleon returned to France in secret as a broken man.

Kutuzov never gave up his goal; he simply chose a smarter, more powerful path. One of letting go. He simply didn't meet force with force. Had he followed his officers' opinion and met Napoleon with traditional resistance, Kutuzov would have been crushed by him.

You and I are commanders too, facing daily battles. Sometimes your "enemy" is a disease. Are you sure you're stronger than it? If not, Kutuzov's strategy may be the wiser one: Let go. Don't resist.

Letting go is not the same as giving up your goal (for example, health). Kutuzov never stopped aiming to expel Napoleon. It's about not falling for the same mistake so many make—applying rigid, linear thinking in situations where flexibility is required. The only time brute force wins is when your opponent is weaker.

But letting go? That strategy works every time.

5. No obsession with the goal.

Focusing obsessively on your goal means holding on. It narrows your thinking and restricts your intelligence. Obsessive concentration means exclusion—you stop noticing what's happening around you. And that blinds you to opportunities.

A salesperson who is obsessed with closing a deal stops really seeing the customer—everyone loses.

Yes, the goal should be there. But if you focus too hard on it, you miss the present moment. And the present is where your intelligence operates.

Athletes show us this clearly. Those who focus too much on winning become tense, and that tension kills performance. They might manage some wins, but they'll never be champions.

One of my seminar participants shared a story that illustrates this. He played tennis with his father and desperately wanted to win. He believed he was in better shape and should beat him. But he kept losing. The more he tried, the more tense he became. Then one day, he gave up the fight. He stopped trying to win and just played. From that day on, he never lost again.

The resistance was gone. Life could flow. The **CURRENT** State shifted to the **TARGET** State.

What's true in sports applies everywhere: in business, in parenting, in employment, in relationships. It's always the same mechanism that's at work. The more you cling to a goal, the more you limit your potential. Let it go.

6. No doubt about the goal.

Doubt comes from the head, and it shuts down universal intelligence. Doubt is the opposite of trust. And without trust, you can't let go.

Letting go means trusting life and the vast wisdom within you.

Without trust, you cling to everything and everyone. That mistrust creates an action and, as we know, every action creates a reaction. If you don't trust life, don't expect life to support you.

Want to reach a goal while doubting? Your chances will be poor. You're blocking the flow. And if you do succeed, it'll take far more energy and time than necessary.

Jesus understood this well: "If you have faith, nothing will be impossible for you."

When you let go (have faith/trust), you allow life to flow and your universal intelligence to manifest, which some call supra-consciousness. Others call it God.

In summary, letting go isn't weakness, it's power. It unlocks the unimaginable intelligence within each one of us by:

Accepting the **CURRENT** state.

Not judging or condemning.

Not obsessing over the path.

Not fighting against the **CURRENT** state or for the **TARGET** state.

Not clinging to the goal.

Not doubting the outcome.

Letting go is how you move with life, not against it. And in that flow, everything becomes possible.

2.3 Avoiding Energy Loss and Energy Blockages

You can't achieve goals without energy. You can't solve problems without energy. And when your energy is low, everything takes longer and feels harder. So we must ask ourselves: Where am I losing energy? Where am I blocking it?

I approach a person's energy situation in a very practical way. I don't differentiate between energy loss and energy blockage. In some cases, we're simply missing a certain amount of energy. And when energy is missing, potential is limited.

So, where and how do we lose or block energy?

The following list doesn't claim to be complete, but it will show you just how "leaky" most people are, like a sieve.

1. We lose or block energy when we don't accept the **CURRENT** state. If we're unable to accept people, situations, our own feelings, or our past, we waste massive amounts of energy. We create inner conflict, and as we've already seen, conflict blocks energy.

2. We lose or block energy when we judge. Judgment divides, and every division creates conflict, which drains energy, just like point 1.

What we're really talking about here is letting go. Letting go is always a matter of life or death. Judgment (separation) leads to death. What is divided is no longer whole. What is not whole cannot grow, unfold, or thrive. Non-judgment is unity, and unity is life.

We all know a perfect example. What happens when male and female merge into one, when the duality is overcome? Life is created. Human beings literally create life by not judging! If we lived in full separation between men and women, humanity would have gone extinct within a century. Life is unity. Separation is death.

From an energy perspective, judgment blocks energy and, therefore, blocks life.

Take a top athlete who constantly criticizes himself. He limits his own potential. Nick Faldo, once ranked world #1 in golf, was such a case. A perfectionist, always dissatisfied with his performance, always judging himself. Eventually, Faldo learned to accept imperfect shots and stopped judging. And what happened? He started playing in a trance and got closer to the perfection he had chased for so long. Perfection isn't achieved by force. It's achieved by letting go. In sports, this is easy to see.

Letting go also dissolves fear of failure, which brings us to the next point.

3. We lose or block energy when we're afraid of failure. Do you remember what I said about curling? A stone thrown with fear is called a "fear stone." Fear can paralyze us completely. When you're paralyzed, you can't use your energy. Fear locks things down; life can't flow.

And as we saw in point 2, the more we judge ourselves, the more fear we generate. Fear of not meeting our own expectations. This creates yet another conflict between the **CURRENT** state and the **TARGET** state. And that conflict drains energy and blocks life.

It always comes back to the same thing: conflict vs. non-conflict, resistance vs. non-resistance.

4. We lose or block energy when we compare. This is a variation of judgment. Those who compare usually end up judging. If you compare your car with your neighbor's car and keep thinking theirs is nicer, you're draining energy.

Interestingly, there is evidence indicating that comparison is common among individuals with cancer. Constant comparison leads to massive energy blockages. And when the body is stuck like that, it often uses illness as a way to break out. Once again, life (letting go) versus death (holding on).

If you want to unlock your full potential, I urge you to stop comparing yourself to others. Not even to your competitors. You are you. Others are others. Each of us has our own life to master.

5. We lose or block energy when we harbor oppressive emotions. When we're angry at someone, we give them power over us. And we lose energy. This is not a useful strategy.

Anger, at its core, is simply non-acceptance of another person. The effects are the same as with judgment and resistance.

Let's look at the Swiss national ski team at the 1992 Winter Olympics in Albertville. Some athletes openly criticized the slopes and showed mixed feelings about them. Their performance was dismal. Unsurprisingly so, they violated fundamental life principles.

Meanwhile, Italian skiing legend Alberto Tomba had no hesitation, no doubt, just fun. And his gold medals spoke for themselves.

It's remarkable how often these principles are overlooked, even at the highest level of sports competition. Fitness and technique are not enough. True champions live by universal laws, and that's what makes them unstoppable.

6. We lose or block energy when we fight. Whether we're fighting for a goal or against a **CURRENT** state, it always creates tension, and tension drains energy.

Here's another sports story: At the 1992 European Soccer Championship, Germany faced Denmark. Germany was the favorite, considered technically and physically stronger. They prepared intensely. Denmark? They relaxed by the sea. And Denmark won. With roughly equal skill and fitness, the team that can let go will always win. Their energy flows better.

But this principle applies far beyond sports.

Take sales. In over 25 years in business, I've never seen a top-performing salesperson who fights hard for their numbers. I've seen many average salespeople who were "hard-working." And I've seen exceptional ones who, without exception, had mastered letting go.

I once led a team of about thirty salespeople. Occasionally, we had to let someone go for missing their targets. These were always the hard workers, the ones who were fighting. But here's what shocked me: During their notice period, many of them suddenly started selling. And not just once, this happened several times.

Why? Because they stopped fighting. They accepted the situation. They stopped judging their performance or sales goals. They just worked. And in doing so, they applied the highest art of Zen Buddhism: Equanimity.

But our motivation systems are designed for the opposite: they motivate a few and demotivate the rest.

Yes, pressure can boost results, but that depends on what you're comparing. If the baseline is low, pressure works. But if you compare two equally skilled teams, one that struggles and one that follows the LO^{2}LA Principle, the difference is obvious.

Like Germany vs. Denmark. The team that fights has no chance; they block not just their intelligence but their energy, too.

In business, this difference can make or break a company. The "flow team" achieves more with less effort. And in today's economy, where so many are playing hardball, that's a huge advantage.

7. We lose or block energy when we feel guilty. Guilt over past actions creates powerful blockages. It prevents us from solving problems quickly, reaching goals efficiently, and accessing our full energy.

In fact, many people with intense guilt also suffer from back pain. They're carrying a heavy load, dragging themselves through life with it. Their posture often shows it. It's like placing a ton of rocks into your car just to make sure you never go fast. It's absurd what people do to themselves, just to avoid being "too comfortable" or successful.

Some even see it as noble to crawl through life with their face in the dirt. Honestly, I don't see anything noble about that.

If you're feeling guilty, drop that weight. Picture yourself tossing it off a cliff.

You only feel guilt when you judge your past. Stop judging it. You've never made a mistake; you've only learned.

And this is not philosophy. It's physics. Who willingly hauls a giant weight around? And who has the right to force you to do so? Only you. Suppose that's what you want, fine. But know that it's your choice.

We've now looked at some of the most common energy leaks and blocks. And they all share one thing: holding on. Holding on drains energy. Letting go allows energy to flow.

As we saw in the last chapter, letting go also activates the universal intelligence that lives in all of us. So now we know that letting go does two things: It prevents energy loss, and it activates intelligence.

That's amazing. One single behavior develops the two most important aspects of our potential: intelligence and energy. That's what I call effective. Let go, and you activate both.

Let me share how I discovered letting go. It helped me meet and marry my wife in record time.

My **CURRENT** state was "no woman." My goal was "the right woman." So, I searched. I dated. I looked everywhere. Nothing lasted. I grew frustrated. Eventually, I stopped looking. Enough was enough.

Three months later, I went on vacation to Tunisia. In November. Not exactly the time or place to meet someone. So I had zero expectations. On a Sahara tour with some French tourists, I met a young woman who struck up a conversation. I didn't think anything about it at first, but as the days passed, we connected.

Two weeks later, back home, I knew she was the one. I flew to Paris a few times, and four months later, we were married.

Yes, people thought I was crazy. She's nine years younger. It would never last, they said. But here we are, nearly fifty years later, and I still know she's the one.

But what's more interesting than how we met is why it worked.

Because I had let go.

I had accepted being single. I accepted the **CURRENT** state, so I stopped fighting for the goal and against what was. And the fight ended. The energy drain ended, too.

I stopped judging single life as "bad." That removed the conflict between now and my goal and let life flow. It freed me.

After all, obsessive focusing means ignoring everything else around you, closing yourself off to possibilities. I didn't give up on my goal; I just stopped clinging to it. It was still inside me, but I trusted life to unfold. And it did, beautifully.

I no longer had doubts. When you're in doubt, your energy passes right through you. Doubt only arises when you're stuck in conflict. Letting go removed that from me.

With minimal effort and in no time, I had "found" the right person. Although really, I hadn't found her, I wasn't even looking.

That's why I now often say: *He who seeks will not find.*

This holds true when the search is full of fear, doubt, judgment, and tension because all of that is holding on and holding on blocks.

But there's a different kind of search. A search without searching.

Real champions do this; successful salespeople do this. And if you're job hunting, you should too. Search by letting go, with deep trust. Trust in life. In your inner intelligence. In God, whatever word fits for you.

It doesn't matter whether you're looking for a job, a client, a house, a car, or an employee. This is the exact process to follow if you want to reach your goals quickly and with ease. And in the next chapter, we'll explore how to take this even further.

2.4 A Surprising Discovery: The Ideal State of Living

"Nothing was, nothing will be; everything is, everything has essence and presence."
—Hermann Hesse, Siddhartha

Technically, we could wrap up the topic of letting go right here. We've covered the most important behaviors and their consequences. But there's something deeper at work, something fundamental that connects all these behaviors.

So, let's ask ourselves: what do all these energy-draining habits, like non-acceptance, judgment, and struggle, have in common?

Let's find out with a few examples:

Not accepting: This means I'm resisting what is right now. I want things to be different, maybe like they used to be or how I imagine them, but not how they are now.

Comparing: I compare the now with the past, with an imagined future, or myself here with someone over there.

Feeling guilty: That's the past holding the present hostage.

Do you see where this is going? Every single one of these behaviors has one thing in common: they're rooted in clinging, come from head-thinking, and reflect an inability to live in the here-and-now. Which means: Anyone who cannot live in the here-and-now wastes energy, blocks energy, and limits their intelligence.

Put positively, letting go is nothing more, and nothing less, than: The ability to live in the here-and-now.

Not being able to live in the moment means rejecting what is and escaping into the past or future. But life doesn't happen in the past. And it doesn't happen in the future. Life only happens now. So the most powerful thing you can do is accept the now.

When you align with the present, you're no longer in conflict with life, and that means: You gain access to the full scope of your intelligence and energy.

Think of it like an electric circuit. If people are like resistors, where does energy (life) flow most freely? Through the person with the least resistance. And who offers the least resistance?

The person who lives fully in the here-and-now.

The moment you step out of the now, you create resistance. And that resistance blocks energy, slows down results, and disrupts problem-solving.

It's pure physics. Living in the present is the most energy-efficient state you can be in. It minimizes resistance and maximizes flow.

Let me add that this "ideal state" can be amplified even more, something we'll explore in the chapter on **Love**. And it's worth noting that physicists have been chasing the dream of superconductivity, that is, energy transmission without resistance. What they're trying to achieve in science, a person can achieve through living in the here and now. Living in the here-and-now is human superconductivity.

If I, as the captain of my ship (my mind), have already set the destination, I no longer need to dwell on the past or worry about the future. The best thing I can do is to stay fully present, trusting that whatever is happening right now is serving the path toward my goal. My universal intelligence knows the destination. It also knows the best way to get there.

I should stop interfering with my limited "head-thinking."

Letting go means: Living in the present moment.

It means letting go of the small self (ego, head-thinking, first reality) so the greater self (heart-thinking, second reality, the divine) can take over.

Other traditions describe this same idea in different terms. In Zen Buddhism, it's called unintentionality—acting without personal intention. Zen practice aims to dissolve the ego, to stop mental interference, and to reach a state of pure, effortless action. That's why Zen strives for non-thinking.

Laozi put it perfectly: "When nothing is done, nothing is left undone."

When I think of how I met my wife, all I can say is: how true, how incredibly true. There is nothing more to do.

Or consider the ideas of the German Catholic priest and mystic Meister Eckhart. He suggested that by attaching ourselves to our own ego, we stand in our own way and cannot bear fruit, cannot fully realize ourselves.

He said this around the year 1300, centuries before modern management discovered the concept of human potential. And yet, most leaders today still do the exact opposite. They cling to their egos and fight tooth and nail, not realizing they are, quite literally, standing in their own way.

You know that expression, "In the land of the blind, the one-eyed man is king?" Heaven help us if ever a two-eyed man emerges.

Eckhart was calling for exactly what we are exploring: the release of the small, limited ego so the universal intelligence within each of us can fully express itself.

But here's the thing: We already live in the here-and-now, at least in certain areas of life. Take breathing, for instance. I've never seen anyone breathe "ahead of time." Breathing only happens now. And it does so with full trust that there will be a next breath.

Or think about playing music. No musician plays a note for the sake of the next note. Every note exists for its own sake. Each note is a moment—a now. And yet, in our lives, we treat almost nothing this way. We're always doing something today because we want something tomorrow. That mindset throws us out of the present, and the resistance begins.

From that point on, we grasp at everything, clinging to whatever gives us the illusion of security. Because outside the present, life feels deeply uncertain. The ice could crack beneath us at any moment. The ceiling might collapse. We buy insurance for everything. The future, as projected by our minds, is dangerous.

And don't forget, whatever the mind can imagine tends to happen (see the chapter on Action = Reaction).

Despite insurance plans and healthy bank accounts, one thing is certain: There is no real security outside the here-and-now. Everything is fragile. A market crash, a pandemic, a natural disaster, a sudden illness, and the illusion of control and security evaporates.

There is only one true security, and it lives within each of us. That security is found by living in the here-and-now. And even the slightest deviation from it can unravel everything.

I can't end this chapter any better than by sharing a short note my wife once scribbled on the back of her grocery list, spontaneously, from the heart:

Total Trust

I have the greatest security there is. Trust. It protects me completely.

Never compare one life with another. Everyone has their lessons to learn.

Material security does not exist if you do not trust in the total protection of your inner God.

From our trust in life, from our knowing that nothing, absolutely nothing, "bad" can happen to us, the abundance of life arises.

It is enough to live, to love every moment, and not to ask questions about the coming moment.

2.5 The Meaning of Life

Some people spend years searching for the meaning of life. A course participant once shared a wonderful story with me on this topic, and I'd like to pass it on to you.

Finding the Meaning of Life in the Kitchen

She had a friend who smoked weed. One time, in an "elevated" state, the friend was struck by a powerful epiphany: she felt she suddenly understood everything and had discovered the meaning of life. Not wanting to lose this insight under any circumstances, she rushed into the kitchen and jotted it down on a piece of paper.

Then she returned to the bedroom. Later, when the effects of the weed had worn off, she eagerly went back into the kitchen to see what profound truth she had written. She found the note and read: "I'm sitting in the kitchen writing."

You can probably imagine the look of astonishment on her face. That's the meaning of life?

But in a way, yes. "I'm sitting in the kitchen writing" is simply another way of saying: I'm fully present in the here-and-now. It's the same message Zen Buddhists have been teaching for centuries: "When I eat, I eat. When I drink, I drink. When I read, I read."

Living in the present moment.

You don't need drugs to discover this truth. A little physics and common sense will do. Life really is that simple—if we focus on what matters.

3. Love

"It seems to me, Govinda, that love is the most important thing in the world. It may be important to great thinkers to examine the world, to explore it, and despise it. But I think it is only important to love the world, not despise it; not for us to hate each other, but to be able to regard the world and ourselves and all beings with love, admiration, and respect."

—Hermann Hesse, Siddhartha

3.1 Love Is

"Harmony, knowledge of the eternal perfection of the world, smiles, unity."

—Hermann Hesse, Siddhartha

There is hardly a concept we have a more complicated relationship with than love. More than 2,000 years of Christianity—the religion centered on love—haven't led to a true understanding of what love really is. I mention Christianity specifically because if any group should grasp the concept of love, it would be Christians. And yet, time and again, I've seen how deeply misunderstood love remains.

During seminars, I've watched participants debate for over an hour, joking, deflecting, and sidestepping, after I had spoken seriously about love for just a few minutes. With a smirk and a pat on the back, someone would inevitably say: "So now we all have to love each other." And the joke was always about love. Strange. Very strange.

Some workshop participants suggest replacing the word love with softer, more agreeable alternatives like harmony, compassion, or understanding. Sure, you can do that. But I can't. Love is love. Period.

It's remarkable how easily we talk about hate, war, even murder, but when it comes to love, we squirm. We bend over backward to avoid using the word. Somehow, it feels offensive. What kind of world do we live in where love feels more awkward to discuss than hate?

People sometimes ask me, "What is love, really? Does it even exist?" In this chapter, I want to offer an answer. More than that, I want to show you what love is capable of.

Earth is the planet of love. That's what we're here to learn, nothing else. Every experience, every challenge, every moment of our lives is designed to move us in one direction: toward more love. Just like in school, some of us learn faster, others slower. And those who don't learn the lesson? They repeat the class. Our entire school system is simply a reflection of this larger spiritual education.

Without love, nothing works. The universe would fall apart. Science now confirms what mystics have always said: everything is interconnected. Everything is one. And this oneness is what we call love. Love is a felt sense of unity. It is the opposite of separation. Separation breeds fear. That's why love is the opposite of fear.

Which brings us full circle, back to what we discussed earlier in this book. From fear to love. If someone claims fear is necessary, they're really saying that the absence of love is necessary. But that's not true because Love, not fear, is the fundamental law of life.

Love is unity. And unity is always stronger than division. Which means: Love is stronger than fear. Put another way: Love is the strongest force in the universe.

This isn't just a belief. It's a reality. And I encourage you not to argue about it, but to test it. Love is like a light switch. We can stand around for hours talking about whether it works, but we only find out by flipping it on.

If love truly is the strongest force in the universe, then it follows that there is no problem that cannot be solved with enough love. And that is exactly what I've seen, time and again. Whether it's personal challenges or global crises, poverty, addiction, violence, or unemployment, love could resolve them all. If we truly wanted to.

And when we focus on healing our own lives, that's not selfish. Why? Because everything is ONE. Solving your personal problems also contributes to solving the world's problems. That's just simple logic.

Earlier, I said that human potential is made up of two things: intelligence and energy. And we talked about how we block and lose energy. Now we complete the picture: Love leads to a maximum of energy and intelligence. Love is the one energy in the universe that can generate itself. That makes it unlimited. And the more love we embody, the more energy we have. And the more energy we have, the faster we can solve problems, reach goals, and realize our potential.

Letting go helps prevent energy loss. Love helps generate energy in abundance.

Activating a maximum of love leads to a maximum of human potential. Jesus or Buddha had such extraordinary human potential as they were living embodiments of pure love. Conversely, where there is hatred or fear, our potential is at its lowest.

Every thought of love increases your potential and adds energy to the universe.

I hope you're beginning to feel how simple everything becomes. At the heart of it all is love. That's why I believe we should be investing in understanding love, not just studying atomic energy or other physical forces. According to Mahatma Gandhi: "The law of love is a far greater science than any modern science."

Yet we still don't treat love as a science. There are no research funds, no institutes, no labs. Why? Because everyone thinks they already know what love is. But if we really understood love, what it is, how it works, what it can do, then our world wouldn't be so full of conflict.

Because where there is love, there is unity. And where there is unity, there is no conflict. And where there is no conflict, there is no resistance.

If you're faced with a problem or goal, and you're choosing between a path of greater resistance or less resistance, the choice should be obvious. But in real life, we often choose the harder road. We fight, we resist, we struggle.

The path of least resistance is the path of love.

Love generates no resistance. And because of that, it is the most direct path to any goal.

We often believe that fighting is the fastest way to solve problems. But that's a short-sighted illusion. A superficial take. Fighting might bring short-term wins, but over time, it creates new problems. And because fighting is loud and dramatic, we're drawn to it. It grabs our attention. Love, by contrast, is quiet. But it works.

Laozi understood this well: "He who defends with love will be secure; Heaven will save him, and protect him with love."

This brings to mind the Japanese martial art Aikido, which I mentioned earlier. A well-trained Aikidoka is, in many ways, virtually unbeatable. One of Aikido's core principles is not to view the aggressor as an enemy, but to remain grounded in unity rather than division. At its heart, this is an expression of love.

This is why Aikido's founder, O-Sensei Morihei Ueshiba, could confidently say that he always "won," even against the strongest of opponents. He understood that true victory is not about defeating another person, but about overcoming the spirit of discord within ourselves. If we hold onto conflict internally and see others as enemies, we've already lost before the battle begins.

If you believe in enemies, you've already lost. Because love knows no enemies. Love knows no conflict.

Let me add something important on the topic of love. When I speak of love in this book, I mean unconditional love—the kind that doesn't set conditions like, "I'll love you if you do this or that." It is love that simply loves, that doesn't judge or divide, because it recognizes that everything is ONE. And if everything is ONE, then everything is God. And if everything is God, then we have every reason to love all things unconditionally.

There is nothing but God. And God is love. And love is absolute security. Fear is man-made insecurity.

We have free will. And so, every moment, we get to choose: Love (strength) or fear (weakness).

My recommendation? Through your willingness, against all logic, against all habit, against all defenses, against all outdated beliefs, against many prevailing doctrines, **choose love.**

Walk in this light, and truly, nothing "bad" can ever happen to you.

There is a quote attributed to the Buddha on the subject of love and helping others: "You must love yourself before you love another. By accepting yourself and fully being what you are, your simple presence can make others happy."

Why? Because everything is ONE. Love knows no boundaries. When you help yourself through love, you help the world through love.

This is the most powerful, cost-effective, and direct way to be of service.

It's far easier to give a donation than to send out five minutes of genuine, unconditional love. But if unconditional love were really that easy, everyone would do it, and the world would already be transformed. So let's make it simple:

Love is unlimited energy.

Love is the strongest force in the universe.

Love is stronger than struggle.

Love gives absolute security.

Love is unity, not separation.

Love is the answer to every question.

Love is the solution to every problem.

The only reason we haven't fully realized this truth is because of our level of consciousness.

3.2 The Path from Social to Universal Consciousness

When I speak of consciousness, I mean everything we are conscious of.

For example, we're conscious that we age. We're conscious that there's a lot of aggression in the world. We're conscious that driving can be dangerous. These are all examples of what I call social consciousness. And social consciousness is often dominated by fear, doubt, mistrust, criticism, conflict, hatred, and thoughts of illness, accidents, aging, and death.

This is why we sometimes call people narrow-minded—they only perceive a tiny sliver of life's possibilities. Their consciousness is narrow.

The more expanded our consciousness, the easier it is to achieve our goals and solve our problems because we can see more, understand more, and respond more intelligently. In fact, more consciousness simply means more intelligence. And intelligence, along with energy, is one of the two components of human potential.

So, our aim should be to expand our consciousness as much as possible. The widest expansion we can imagine is what I call universal consciousness. This means being aware of the universe as a whole. Since everything is ONE, as we've seen, universal consciousness reflects the unity of all life. This is the most we can possibly achieve.

So, how do we move from narrow consciousness to a much broader one?

The answer is simple: love.

Love expands consciousness. Fear and hate contract it. If you picture consciousness as a tall glass vase, then social consciousness sits at the bottom and universal consciousness at the top. Love lifts us upward. Fear pulls us down. If we want to rise above our problems and worries, if we want to fly, then there's only one answer: more love.

Back in Chapter 3.1, I said that Earth is the planet of love. This lines up with the ideas of the French priest and scientist, Teilhard de Chardin, and even modern nuclear physics. For Teilhard, everything evolves toward what he called the "Omega Point," a state of complete consciousness and unity, which we could call universal consciousness. Nuclear physicist Jean-Emile Charon said the same: everything evolves toward more consciousness. And since more consciousness is more love, everything, humans, animals, plants, is evolving toward love.

This understanding of consciousness has big consequences.

First: every human being already contains the full range of possibilities, from the narrowest to universal consciousness. These are latent within us, waiting to be recognized and brought to light. Love is the key that unlocks them. Every time we reject a person or a situation, we block ourselves from moving to a higher level of consciousness.

So, the most powerful thing we can do for our own growth is to love whatever happens to us. This is the fastest path to development.

I urge you never to forget this. Personally, I don't understand how so many so-called "experts" talk about personal development without ever mentioning love.

Second: anything that exists in your consciousness as a real possibility can happen in your life. And here's the deeper truth:

What does not exist in your consciousness as a possibility cannot happen.

Imagine that. If the idea of aggression didn't exist in your consciousness, you could never become the "victim" of aggression. But the moment even the smallest thought of it enters your awareness, the door opens. You create the potential for it to occur.

And the same is true in reverse. If your consciousness is filled only with the idea of love, then "bad" things can't happen to you. Life can only give you what your consciousness allows.

So I ask you: "What's in your consciousness?"

If your thoughts include illness, accident, failure, or recession, then these are possible outcomes. If not, then they're not. It's that simple.

There once lived an older Catholic priest in New York who routinely walked alone through one of the city's worst neighborhoods at night. And nothing ever happened to him. Why? Because he had not a single thought of fear or danger. He was completely immersed in love. And if love truly is the strongest force in the universe, as we've said, what could possibly harm him?

Remember: nothing happens by chance. You don't get attacked "by accident." That kind of event only happens if the thought of attack or aggression exists inside you. Sadly, because most people carry these thoughts, such things are statistically likely. It's just a matter of time.

If something isn't in your consciousness, it cannot become part of your experience.

Imagine two people traveling to the same city. One believes it's dangerous, the other believes it's safe and beautiful. They will each experience what they expect. And both will be right.

As Jesus said: "May it be done to you according to your faith." If you replace "faith" with "consciousness," it becomes: It happens to you according to what's in your consciousness.

Ask yourself: Is your consciousness filled with love, or with fear, aggression, and defense?

It's also true that people with similar levels of consciousness tend to attract one another. So, your encounters aren't random; you're meeting people who resonate with how you think and feel.

Look around. Some people carry a consciousness of poverty; others carry one of wealth. And again, "be it done unto you according to your faith"—they get exactly what they expect. That's why poverty can't be solved by handing out food alone (as the Buddha reminded us). Real change only comes by changing consciousness. That's the kind of help that transforms lives.

Everything is a question of consciousness.

If you're angry with someone, you remain attached to them. To free yourself, you have to change your consciousness. Love them or accept them as they are, and you detach from them, both emotionally and spiritually.

Let me repeat the most important advice in this chapter: Whatever happens, love it.

Why? Because love expands consciousness. It allows you to create what you want faster and more easily. Love means no conflict. No resistance. Which means life can flow at full speed. When we don't love, we block our development. We block our intelligence, our energy, and our potential. And we expose ourselves to all kinds of unnecessary difficulties, aggression, insecurity, and misfortune. No matter how "bad" the world may seem, someone who carries enough love in their consciousness will not be affected by it. Your only limit is your lack of love.

Earlier, I said human potential is unlimited. This is one more reason why. If love has no limit, then neither does your potential. And how could love ever be limited?

But to access this, we have to wake up from the common dream of social consciousness. We have to stop thinking about what everyone else thinks. We have to stop trying to be "nice" just to please others or avoid conflict. We have to think for ourselves regardless of what our parents, schools, neighbors, or the media have told us. That's what it means to grow up in our thinking.

What others think of you is irrelevant. What you think of others matters because everything is ONE, and the world reflects what you believe about it. But even more important is this: What you think of yourself.

3.3 Love Your Neighbor as Yourself

This sentence will probably be familiar to every Christian: Love your neighbor as yourself. In my experience, though, most people focus almost entirely on the first part. Yet I believe the second part is far more important. Why?

Because if you don't love yourself, you can't truly love others.

Earlier, I explained why it's essential to love everything that happens to us, both people and situations. But to do that, we need something first: love for ourselves. Self-love. This has nothing to do with selfishness as long as we remember that everyone else is just as lovable as we are.

According to the LO²LA Principle, the most important quality for a leader is this: the ability to love themselves. If they don't, they won't be able to love their employees, and if they can't love them, they can't truly lead them. Instead, they'll bring their own unresolved issues into the workplace with all the usual negative consequences. A person who loves themselves is in harmony with themselves. And someone who is in harmony won't bring conflict into the world.

We also saw earlier that love leads to expanded consciousness and that consciousness is directly tied to knowledge. We've all heard the saying: Know thyself. But how do you come to truly know yourself? How do you discover your full potential?

There's only one answer: by loving yourself.

Yet what do many people do in order to better understand themselves? They analyze themselves, or let others analyze them. But based on everything we've covered so far, this isn't the best path to self-knowledge. Self-analysis is often a symptom of a lack of self-love. Someone who truly loves themselves doesn't need to be dissected. Analysis breaks things down into separate parts and rarely produces better results than simple love for oneself. In fact, people who are analyzed often end up fixating on their weaknesses instead of their strengths.

Please keep this clearly in mind: Analysis divides, and where division exists, conflict follows. Love unites, and where unity exists, there is peace.

From a purely logical standpoint, love is far superior to analysis. And it's much faster and less expensive.

That makes love not just more powerful, but also more economical. Imagine the implications for a business: hundreds or even thousands of employees either expressing or suppressing love. The potential that's either released or blocked is enormous.

I knew of a company that spent a great deal of time analyzing its employees, trying to identify strengths and weaknesses to promote top performers. But the company struggled. Why? Because the employees became focused on their shortcomings rather than their strengths, which is the opposite of self-love. The damage caused by this approach was enormous.

Then there was another company, one that never even considered analyzing its employees. The leadership mindset was simple: We love our employees. This attitude naturally unlocked their potential. The result? Above-average growth within just a few years.

Consider this, too: Someone who loves themselves also loves the entire world, through themselves and within themselves. Why? Because everything is ONE.

At the beginning of this book, I said I was pursuing a single question: How can we get from where we are to where we want to be with the least time and effort?

We saw that this requires two things: intelligence and energy. And now we've discovered what leads to maximum intelligence and energy: love. And because everything begins with the self, we can refine the answer even further: Love for yourself.

So, the clear answer to the central question becomes: Loving yourself (and others) is the fastest and most effortless path to achieving any goal.

Take losing weight as an example. There is no easier or more affordable way to lose weight than loving yourself. That means accepting yourself fully, including the extra weight.

The same goes for a salesperson. There is no simpler, quicker, or more effective way to sell than loving yourself. From this foundation grows love for your customers, and, naturally, love for your product.

And the same applies to someone who is sick. There is no faster or more cost-effective way to support healing than self-love. Please note: I'm not saying you shouldn't see a doctor.

I'm saying that love enhances the healing process in ways we can hardly imagine. I could give countless examples, and every single one would show the same thing.

The nuclear physicist Jean-Émile Charon, whom I've quoted several times already, put it best: "Love is the simplest and most effective process for increasing knowledge in the universe." There is nothing simpler than love. There is nothing more powerful than love.

Let that sink in. How elegantly simple the world—the entire universe—is designed. Love is the source of it all.

This is the most radical and economical principle that exists. Love is not just a mystical feeling; it's applied economics and physics. That is why the following statement is so powerful: "Love your neighbor as yourself."

It is one of the most extraordinary principles ever discovered in physics. This is superconductivity in its purest and most practical form.

But be careful with the word neighbor. Because if everything is ONE, then everyone is our neighbor. Not just people, but everything, animals, plants, even stones. As we established earlier, everything has consciousness, including stones and plants.

The first time I consciously practiced this principle was during a period of intense conflict with employees, customers, and suppliers. Every evening, I came home drained. Conflict takes energy. It wears you down, physically, emotionally, mentally. I didn't know what to do, at least not through conventional means. So I had to take a radically different approach. That approach was love.

Here's what I did: I told myself, *If I can spend a few minutes every day on my physical hygiene, why not also spend a few minutes on my mental hygiene?* I started spending five minutes every morning silently sending love to the people I was in conflict with. I simply imagined them and sent them love.

A few days later, I realized: if I have five minutes in the morning, I have five in the evening too. So, I added another session. Eventually, I found myself doing it more than twice a day.

The results were astonishing. After about three months, all the conflicts had resolved peacefully and to everyone's satisfaction.

This kind of conflict resolution doesn't leave anyone behind. There are no losers, only winners. Because when someone walks away from a conflict feeling defeated, that unresolved energy doesn't disappear. It reappears elsewhere as another conflict.

One man once told me about a similar experience. He often had to attend board meetings, and by the end, he always felt completely drained. Then one day, he tried a new strategy. He didn't say a single word during the entire meeting. He just sat there silently thinking: *I love you.* The results stunned him. After the meeting, two colleagues came up to thank him for what he'd "said." He hadn't spoken at all. And yet they felt heard, uplifted. And so did he.

Remember: when you send love to someone, you're also sending love to yourself and the whole world because everything is ONE.

It doesn't matter who the love is directed toward; it always benefits the entire universe.

And that means you're also helping to bring peace, even to global military conflicts. That's not a small thing.

What's the best thing you can do to help resolve the world's conflicts? Love yourself. And love others.

3.4 The Cause of All Human Problems and How to Overcome Them

Based on everything we've discussed so far, the answer to this next question should be clear: What is the root cause of all human problems?

It is the belief in separation and division.

As we've seen, this belief is an illusion. There is no real separation in the universe, not between you and me, not between you and others. The idea of separation is false, and it inevitably leads to conflict. And conflict leads to problems.

So why do we cling to this idea of separation? What causes it? The answer is simple: a lack of love.

Love is the experience of unity. When love is missing, the illusion of separation takes over.

Wherever this illusion becomes too strong, problems follow. Just look at the perceived separation between humans and nature. From time to time, we remember that we are part of nature, that we and the natural world form a single, interconnected whole. And when we remember that, even for a moment, our thinking shifts. When you feel one with something, you treat it with care. But when you see it as separate, you treat it as something to control, exploit, or fear.

The same goes for the separation between men and women. When this divide is emphasized too strongly, we create unnecessary conflict. Or take the separation between religions—how many wars have been fought in the name of religious differences? Or the divide between management and employees: when the gap becomes too wide, dysfunction and breakdown are inevitable.

But this separation doesn't originate outside of us. It begins within.

We've created a split inside ourselves between head and heart, between reason and love. We've pushed love aside and elevated rationality as our guiding principle. In doing so, we've lost balance. We've made reason our god, and in the process, created many of the problems we now face.

When we divide ourselves internally, we project that division outward. This reflects a deeper truth: everything is connected. If I am fragmented within, I will see the world as fragmented too.

Many people suffer under this inner division. And when the pain becomes too much to bear, they often turn to drugs. From my perspective, people struggling with drug addiction are highly sensitive individuals searching, often unconsciously, for a sense of wholeness. In this way, they reflect the deeper condition of our society.

The solution to our problems doesn't lie out in the world. It lies within each of us.

To overcome our problems, we must first overcome the illusion of separation. And to do that, we need more love—love for ourselves, for others, for life itself.

Let me repeat it: "Love your neighbor as yourself."

Even from a scientific or economic perspective, there is no better formula.

3.5 Gratitude:
A forgotten dimension

A practical expression of love is gratitude. Only those who have enough love in their hearts can truly be grateful. Where love is lacking, gratitude is missing too. Gratitude, then, is love in action.

In *The World is Sound: Nada Brahma*, Joachim-Ernst Berendt writes beautifully about the connection between music and gratitude: "That is why all music is, first and foremost, praise to God. This idea also pervades the musical traditions of almost all the peoples of the world."

Music is an expression of gratitude, and thus of love. It seems that, deep down, people across cultures have always understood the universal power of love. A lack of gratitude shows a lack of respect for life. And how can we expect life to reward us if we don't honor or appreciate it? Once again, we see the law of Action = Reaction at play.

I often emphasize the practical and even economic side of love, and by extension, gratitude. Let me share a powerful example.

A team of salespeople had a daily goal: 40 sales calls. On average, this led to 4 product demonstrations (they were selling vacuum cleaners), and from those, one sale. But one salesman had a completely different approach, and astonishing results. He made just 12 calls a day, resulting in 6 demos and three sales. In other words, with a third of the effort, he made three times the sales and earned three times the commission.

How is that possible?

As some of you might have guessed, it comes down to the LO²LA Principle, specifically, to love. Most salespeople get frustrated with rejection. As we've seen, frustration and anger drain energy and intelligence, and the results reflect that.

The exceptional salesman did something else entirely. He gave thanks, not just for the sales, but also for the rejections. He inwardly appreciated every conversation, every door opened, every person he met, regardless of the outcome. He loved the whole process and gave thanks for all of it.

Being grateful for a sale is easy. Every average salesperson does that. But being grateful for so-called failures, that's where the real difference lies.

His success wasn't due to special training or secret techniques. It came from a specific internal posture: one of love and gratitude toward life itself.

Those who love life, who give thanks, are rewarded by life. That's just the law of Action = Reaction in motion. In fact, the entire LO²LA Principle is captured in the act of gratitude. Gratitude is a form of letting go. It allows energy to flow and life to shift.

And that's what's needed to reach your goals. Gratitude is one of the purest and most powerful expressions of universal love, simple, practical, and transformative.

The French writer and philosopher Voltaire may have sensed this truth more than 200 years ago. In his famous novel Candide, he touches on gratitude in a way that's hard to beat for its clarity and impact.

Candide visits the mythical land of El Dorado and asks an old man whether the country has a religion. The man replies, "How could we not? Do you think we're ungrateful?" Candide asks which religion they follow. The old man blushes: "Is there more than one? We have the religion of the whole world; we praise God from morning till night."

Candide presses on. Do they worship just one God? "Of course," the man says. "There aren't two or three or four. Honestly, people from your world ask some strange questions."

Candide then asks how they pray or make requests to God. The old man replies, "We don't ask Him for anything. He's already given us everything. All we do is thank Him, endlessly."

Finally, Candide asks where the priests are. The man smiles. "We are all priests," he says. "Every morning, the king and the heads of every family sing hymns of gratitude, accompanied by thousands of musicians."

Remarkable, isn't it?

Voltaire even describes El Dorado's wealth as unimaginable: goblets made of diamonds, streets paved with gold, and precious stones.

So let me be clear: Love and gratitude have nothing to do with weakness or poverty. Quite the opposite. If love is the strongest force in the universe, then it would make no sense for it to lead to lack or limitation. There is no shortage in the universe, only abundance. Love is the source of everything, and love knows no limits. It is human beings, through limited and fearful thinking, who have created poverty and scarcity. In that sense, poverty is a symptom of a lack of love.

Just look around:

Poverty, hunger, illness, addiction, unemployment, war, aggression—these are all consequences of a lack of love and a lack of gratitude.

So how can we hope to solve these problems if we continue to ignore the one thing that truly matters? Without love, any solution is just a surface-level patch. It may offer short-term results, but over time, the problems will only grow. Wherever love is missing, problems will persist and multiply. You don't need to be a prophet to see that.

Please remember: None of this is about religion or belief. These are real-life principles, universal truths you can apply to yourself.

No matter how big your challenges may seem, if you begin *right now* to give thanks for everything that happens to you, your life will begin to shift in ways you never imagined. Within 1 to 3 years, things can change completely. And that timeline depends only on how much conviction and consistency you bring to the practice of gratitude.

Even if it takes three years, what are three years in the course of a life?

Part Four:

Bringing It All Together

1. Summary

I developed the LO^{2}LA Principle in three stages. Not every part is equally important for everyone; what resonates deeply with one person may not matter as much to another. That's why it makes sense for each reader to create a personal summary. Try to distill what matters most to you into a sentence or a few words.

To help you get started, here are a few suggestions of what such a summary might look like:

Option 1: *LO^{2}LA*

Love (squared), Letting go, Action = Reaction

Option 2: *Love your neighbor as yourself.*

Five words that can change your life.

Option 3: *I know. It is simple. I am Love.*

Eight words that can transform your life.

Option 4: *I am responsible.*

This marks a quantum leap in personal development.

Option 5: *NOW*

Living fully in the present moment—the ideal state of being that unleashes the highest levels of universal intelligence and energy (potential).

If you reflect on all these possibilities, you'll likely arrive at the same conclusion: Nothing matters more than what I think NOW.

2. The Big Mistake

Now and then, we come across the concept: "You will be like God." But if we reflect on everything discussed in this book, we must conclude that this sentence isn't quite accurate.

If everything is truly ONE, then that means we are already ONE with God. We are not separate. We are part of the same all-powerful, all-knowing, all-loving force. Therefore, it's not *you will be like God*. It's: *You are God*.

This misunderstanding has serious consequences. The phrase "You will be like God" pushes divinity into some distant future. It suggests that we have a long road ahead before we can even hope to get there. Tragically, this is the strategy used by countless belief systems, methods, and gurus: First, they tell us we're broken or sinful, and then they offer us a long, complicated path to become "like God." And, conveniently, they're the only ones who know the way.

But here's the trick: that goal always stays just out of reach. It's like the old carrot-and-stick metaphor, you chase and chase, but you never arrive. Meanwhile, you're burdened by guilt, effort, and blind trust.

Let me say it clearly: *"You will be like God"* is the surest *guarantee that you never will be.*

Now consider this: In the universe, there is no time. Time is an illusion. Everything—past, present, and future —is happening at once. There is only the now. So, the only possible moment to be God is this one. Not someday. Not after years of effort. Now.

We are God, now. We've forgotten that we are omnipotent, omniscient, and above all, that we are love.

Which means we don't need to become anything. We already are everything. We don't need to learn something new. We need to remember what is already within us. And we need to let go of the crutches—the beliefs, fears, doubts, and dependencies—that keep us from recognizing it.

Perception is closely tied to cognition, and cognition is shaped by consciousness. As we've seen, consciousness expands through love. Every human being is a fountain of love. Not will be, but already is, here and now.

If you're thinking, *But I'm not ready yet,* or *I still need to do more work on myself,* then stop for a moment and remember one of the most powerful principles of life:

The world is what you think it is.

If you believe you still need to spend years improving yourself, that becomes your truth, and so you will. If you believe the journey is long and hard, then it will be long and hard for you.

Don't let yourself be talked out of your own truth, even if a hundred gurus tell you otherwise. (For the record: I have nothing against gurus, I only take issue with becoming dependent on them.)

If you think, *There is no God*, that becomes your truth, and your life will reflect it. If you think, *One day I'll be like God*, then that, too, is your truth, and "one day" will always stay just out of reach. If you think, *I'm a sinner who has to work endlessly on myself*, then you've sentenced yourself to exactly that. But if you think, *I am God*, then that becomes your truth, and the work is done. You have arrived.

The problem with us humans: We keep trying to become something we already are.

We seek God outside ourselves. We attend endless workshops, conferences, and meetings. We read stacks of books, listen to experts, professors, and gurus. All the while, God is already within us, permanently.

If only we would stop trying and start being, we'd awaken to the full truth of who we are. We would experience a clear, direct consciousness of reality.

3. A New Perspective

I'd like to draw your attention once more to the perspective offered by The LO²LA Principle. As I've said throughout this book, my goal is to show you how to move from your **CURRENT** state to your **TARGET** state, as quickly and effortlessly as possible.

Let's briefly review what we've explored so far:

1. Anyone who constantly criticizes or condemns the world and others, who sends out heavy thoughts, will either struggle to reach their goals or only get there with great effort. This approach is inefficient. It drains energy and leads to poor outcomes in business, in politics, in sports, and in personal life.

2. Those who understand the law of Action = Reaction behave differently. They criticize less, judge less, and focus on sending out constructive, positive thoughts. As a result, they achieve their goals faster and with less effort.

3. Those who can let go move forward. Letting go removes resistance, allowing goals to manifest more quickly and with even less struggle.

4. And if you also understand and live according to the law of love, you move even faster. You align with the highest frequency of all, unconditional love, and this opens the flow of life in ways logic alone cannot explain.

The final state, the most powerful and transformative, is the one shown to us by Jesus and other great masters:

The **CURRENT** state IS the **TARGET** state.

In other words, the time between where you are and where you want to be shrinks to zero.

There is no longer a gap between desire and reality. Jesus didn't say, "You will be healed someday." He healed then and there.

What is = What should be. This is the essence of true mastery. The LO^{2}LA Principle is your guide to reaching this state, not just faster, but with more efficiency and less resistance at every step.

The path unfolds in three progressive phases:

1. Action = Reaction
2. Letting go
3. Love

Each step brings you closer to the effortless fulfillment of your goals. This path leads from limited love to ever-expanding love, culminating in unconditional love and with it, universal consciousness.

And now it's up to you. You know the path. You have free will. You can walk the path, or recognize that, in truth, there is no path to walk.

The final insight is this: You've already arrived. You just need to realize it.

In the end, there is only one true goal:

To love what *IS*. This one goal contains all others.

The visual representation of The LO²LA Principle looks as follows:

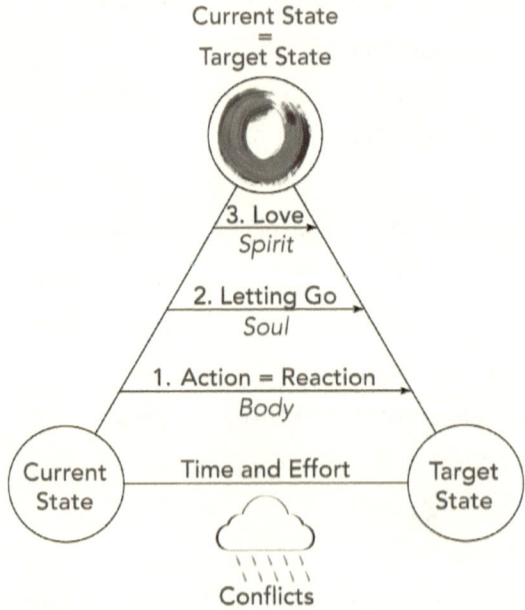

The LO²LA Principle consists of three parts. Human beings also consist of three parts: body, soul, and spirit. Human development, our evolution from the purely physical toward the spiritual, is essentially a movement toward greater love.

You can also visualize goal achievement through this threefold lens:

A person who is strongly attached to the material world, that is, to the body, must exert significant effort to reach their goals. Progress feels slow and heavy because for this person, reality exists only on the dense, physical level. Life becomes a struggle.

Someone who can mentally rise above matter, operating more from the soul, will reach their goals with less effort. Things begin to flow more smoothly, more quickly.

And when a person operates at the level of spirit, which is the level of unconditional love, everything flows with the least effort of all.

Again, the three-part structure of the LO^{2}LA Principle aligns with the three-part nature of the human being: Body, Soul, and Spirit.

But it's important to remember: this isn't about separating one part from the others. Together, they form one whole. Each part complements and depends on the others. And that's exactly what I've aimed to show you throughout this book.

I wish you success as you apply The LO^{2}LA Principle in your own life.

Acknowledgement

I thank the unlimited universal intelligence that moves through me and through all who helped bring this book to life.

Sources

Berendt, Joachim-Ernst. 1985. *The World is Sound: Nada Brahma* Hamburg: Rowohlt Verlag.

Brand, Rolf. 1987. *Aikido*, München: Falken-Verlag.

Charon, Jean E. 1989. *The Fall of Evolution.* Berlin: Ullstein Verlag.

Charon, Jean E.1988. *The Spirit of Matter.* Berlin: Ullstein Verlag.

Charon, Jean E. 1983. *J'ai vécu quinze milliards d'années.* Paris: Albin Michel.

Davies, Paul. 1988. *The Cosmic Blueprint: Principle of Chaos.* München: Goldmann Verlag.

Dürckheim, Karlfried Graf. 1975. *Wonderful Cat and Other Zen Texts.* Leipzig: Otto Wilhelm Barth Verlag.

Ferrucci, Piero. 1922. *Boundless Wealth.* Basil: Sphinx Verlag

Fromm, Erich. 1975. *The Art of Loving.* Zurich: Ex Libris Book Club.

Garaudy, Roger. 1982. *Appeal to the Living.* Zurich: Ex Libris Book Club.

Hartmann, Franz. 1960. *The Bhagavad Gita.* Schatzkammerverlag Hans Fändrich

Hesse, Hermann. 1972. *Siddhartha.* Berlin: Suhrkamp Verlag.

Iqbal, Mohammad. 1989. *Les Secrets du Soi.* Paris. Albin Michel.

Krishnamurti, Jiddu. 1987. *From Darkness to Peace.* Berlin: Ullstein Verlag.

Krishnamurti, Jiddu. 1989. *Breakthrough to Freedom.* Berlin: Ullstein Verlag.

Laozi. 1972. *Tao Te Ching.* Zurich: Ex Libris Book Club.

Lassier, Suzanne. 1970. *Gandhi et la non-violence.* Paris: Éditions du Seuil.

Maturana, Humberto R. & Varela, Francisco J. 1991. *The Tree of Knowledge.* Munich: Goldmann Verlag.

Maurois, André. 1966. *Napoleon.* Hamburg: Rowohlt Verlag.

Murphy, Dr. Joseph. 1993. *La magie de la foi.* Escalquens: Éditions Dangles.

Percheron, Maurice. 1967. *Buddha.* Hamburg: Rowohlt Verlag.

Rifkin, Jeremy. 1985. *Entropie – ein neues* Weltbild. Berlin: Ullstein Verlag.

Roads, Michael J. 1991. *Au cœur de la nature.* Éditions Vivez Soleil.

Rose, Dennis. 1992. *Zen Management.* Escalquens: Éditions Dangles.

Staehelin, Balthasar. 1970. *Die Welt als Du.* Zurich: Ex Libris Book Club.

Tompkins, Peter & Bird, Christopher: 1983. *Das geheime Leben der Pflanzen.* Frankfurt: Fischer.

Voltaire. 1963. *Candide.* Reclam Verlag.

Watts, Alan W. 1978. *Wisdom of Insecurity.* Leipzig: Otto Wilhelm Barth Verlag.

About the Author

René Egli is an economist, author, speaker and lifelong systems thinker whose work bridges spirituality, logic, and human performance. For over 30 years, he has studied the universal mechanisms behind flow, success, and effortless action. His bestseller, The LO²LA Principle, distilled these insights into a formula that has inspired readers around the world. René has since published multiple follow-up works expanding on choice, freedom, and the role of consciousness in daily life. His mission remains the same: to help people understand the underlying order of existence, and to show that when you align with it, conflict dissolves and goals become natural outcomes.

thelolaprinciple.com
lolaprinzip.ch